"Driven by an urgency for the Church to make disciples of all nations, Darre need for evangelistic engagement that reflects a cultural intelligence characterized by conviction, conscientiousness, compassion, and contextualization. It's an important read for all who seek missional effectiveness in these changing times."

—**Claude Alexander**, senior pastor, The Park Church, Charlotte, NC

"Many Christians today are experiencing a 'cultural concussion.' Frustrated that they've lost something from the past and no longer sure of where they are, Christians in the West find themselves grasping to get their bearings and fearful of an uncertain future. Unsure of how to proceed, the temptation for the church is to either 'come out swinging' or retreat to the safe confines of their own communities. *Cultural Intelligence* offers a different way forward, which includes both a cure and a calling: a gospel that connects us to God and transforms our whole lives—not only what we believe, but also who we are, what we say, and how we say it. Darrell Bock is a world-class New Testament scholar with a pastor's heart, a doctor with a bedside manner, who helps us not only get our biblical bearings but also shows us how the church can recalibrate our approach to become a field hospital for sinners."

—**Joshua D. Chatraw**, executive director, Center for Public Christianity, and theologian-in-residence, Holy Trinity Anglican Church

"Dr. Darrell Bock's challenge in *Cultural Intelligence* is a critically needed and gentle course correction for the church in America today if we ever hope to bridge the sacred-secular divide. He convincingly admonishes us from six key New Testament passages to become ambassadors of reconciliation, introducing complicated modern lives to the truth of the Bible, not the other way around, with a gentle and respectful tone. He reminds us that engagement's purpose is to get a hearing for the gospel which offers a despairing culture a powerful hope. Dr. Bock's approach to engaging the American culture, minus the Judeo-Christian safety net, resembles the thoughtful and intentional preparation of a cross-cultural foreign missionary serving in a creative access country."

—**Mike Chupp**, chief executive officer, Christian Medical & Dental Associations

"Darrell Bock addresses in readable fashion the ways in which we have engaged as Christians in culture wars, pointing out that there is little evidence to prove we've won any of them. I often talk about the most effective approach being one of a firm center and soft edges. *Cultural Intelligence* takes this thought and goes deep, giving us the big picture and practical advice on staying biblically rooted (firm center) and engaging with charity (soft edges). Darrell provides an antidote to so many of the ineffective ways in which Christians have navigated the complexities and culture wars of our day, such as firm center and harsh edges or spongy center and soft edges. This book strikes the right balance of being full of grace and truth."

—**Barry H. Corey**, president, Biola University

"Very few people in public life have given more thought to the way our Christian faith influences the way we think about our world more than Darrell Bock. This is why this book is a must-read for pastors, leaders, and anyone wanting to be faithful in this faithless age. Too often we are guilty of simply reacting, based on our partisan sympathies rather than doing the hard work of getting underneath our current debates. You may not agree with every conclusion Dr. Bock makes, but you will come away not only with compelling insights but with intellectual tools to help you think well."

—Daniel Darling, senior VP of communications, National Religious Broadcasters

"Darrell Bock is recognized as one of the finest evangelical biblical scholars of our generation. With the publication of *Cultural Intelligence,* readers are privileged not only to see Bock's keen insights into the meaning of key biblical texts, but to hear Bock's heart as he provides timely application to guide believers toward faithful discipleship in this fallen world in which we live. After providing helpful framing of our current context and culture, Bock calls for individual Christ followers, churches, and the Christian community at-large to engage and renew the culture in a grace-filled manner. Believing that cultural intelligence can only be developed with biblical conviction and Spirit-enabled kindness, Bock encourages believers to prioritize God's reconciling work in the world through Jesus Christ, along with the themes of hope, love, and the transformational power of the gospel. I pray that believers will reflect the fruit of the Spirit called for in Bock's fine work as we all seek to put into practice the author's wise counsel. I am delighted to recommend this thoughtful book."

—David S. Dockery, president, International Alliance for Christian Education; theologian-in-residence, Southwestern Baptist Theological Seminary; and former president, Trinity Evangelical Divinity School

"*Cultural Intelligence* is a much-needed word in our world of hostile, tribal responses. It is rooted in Scripture and full of practical advice for how to engage as believers in our challenging, pluralistic world. It is a needed course correction for how to battle for the faith by pointing to the faith. It suggests how to have conversations of value versus debilitating debate. In short, it is a must read."

—**Tony Evans**, president, The Urban Alternative, and senior pastor, Oak Cliff Bible Fellowship, Dallas, TX

"Christians urgently need to develop sharper cultural intelligence, whether in politics or in Hollywood or in everyone's daily work, and there are few better able to help us than Darrell Bock. This book bridges the gap between deep biblical wisdom and lived experience with the rapidly changing challenge of our culture. Bock provides both a firm scriptural foundation and an up-to-date approach to culture that is truly constructive, rather than destructive or complacent. He demonstrates how to reunite the long-opposed agendas of evangelism and social activism, showing that if we have cultural intelligence grounded in a gospel of reconciliation, we can reconcile these concerns into a fruitful mission for the church in the world."

—**Greg Forster**, director, Oikonomia Network

"All of us as church leaders want to effectively engage our culture, but where do we begin? How do we choose those moments? What aspects of culture do we address first? More than that, which culture are we seeking to engage? In a time when the church is working without the safety of a Judeo-Christian worldview, how do we seek to redeem our fallen cultures? Darrell Bock has provided a biblically grounded and pastorally sensitive guide for Christians to intelligently and compassionately begin those conversations of grace and redemption. This book should be the beginning point of any church or group that is looking for a way to make a difference in the world around them.

No, it doesn't give you all of the answers, but it will guide you to begin to ask the right questions. And we know, that's half of the battle."

—**Mike Glenn**, senior pastor, Brentwood
Baptist Church, Brentwood, TN

"Darrell Bock's book *Cultural Intelligence* is like a gentle rain in a parched land. How should Christians live during this divisive time, where everything is angrily dichotomized by red or blue, Christian or non-believer? Bock answers simply and profoundly, 'People are not the enemy, they are the goal.' *Cultural Intelligence* is a must read for Christ followers who want to engage others in this post-Christian age by honing their listening skills and living biblically based lives of hope."

—**David C. Iglesias**, director, Wheaton Center for Faith,
Politics and Economics, and Jean and E. Floyd Kvamme
Associate Professor of Politics and Law, Wheaton College

"This book is a needed reminder that it is not only necessary for us to speak the truth, but how we speak it matters. Darrell Bock points out that we as Christians have often appeared angry and combative, alienating many people from considering Christianity. From Scripture and personal experiences, he shows that we must hold tightly to the truth, but with a caring and understanding spirit. The better we know our culture and the secular mindset the better we will know how to gain a hearing. I intend to read this book again, and if you read it, I think you will do the same."

—**Erwin W. Lutzer**, pastor emeritus,
The Moody Church, Chicago, IL

"After decades of brilliant scholarship plumbing the depths of the Bible for the benefit of the church, Darrell Bock has focused his formidable abilities on crafting a biblical model for the church's engagement with the world. In *Cultural Intelligence*, Darrell's masterful walk through the key passages that govern engagement with outsiders demonstrates that God cares at least as much about how we communicate as he does what we communicate. I heartily recommend this work which focuses on how to build bridges not barriers and encourages us to see our role as ambassadors involved in cultural engagement rather than culture wars."

> —**Larry Moody**, chaplain, PGA and CPGA Players,
> and president and founder, In the Game Ministries

"Not since the early church has the cultural chasm between Christ-followers and the outside world been this vast. And growing by the day! What we need are relational bridges built with mutual understanding and concern. This requires tact, relational skill, and, in a phrase, 'cultural intelligence.' In this winsome, biblical primer on cultural engagement, Darrell Bock imparts the analytic and relational tools Christians need to live out their sacred calling as salt and light."

> —**Samuel L. Perry**, associate professor of sociology
> and religious studies, University of Oklahoma

"Oh, how Christians need a constructive orientation on how to engage the public square and those with different ideologies and views! Drawing from key scriptural texts and years of experience, Bock recalibrates discussion on how to understand our witness and calling in the world. What is needed is a humble tone, a new entry into the Bible, and the recognition that such a stance can be costly. This is a timely book!"

> —**M. Daniel Carroll R. (Rodas)**, Blanchard Professor of
> Old Testament, Wheaton College and Graduate School

"I am delighted to see *Cultural Intelligence* become available and hope it is widely read. It is thoroughly biblically grounded, and contains a rich reservoir of practical advice on how to engage cultures wisely and winsomely. The final section on teaching the Bible in today's culture is worth the price of the entire book! A must read for church leaders and those interested in meaningfully interacting with the cultural mosaic facing the church today."

—**Scott B. Rae**, senior advisor to the president for university mission, dean of faculty, and professor of philosophy and Christian ethics, Talbot School of Theology, Biola University

"Looking at a time well before the advent of MTV or the Internet, or the ruling in *Roe v. Wade*, Darrell Bock identifies the roots of our social upheaval and cultural war. He navigates the tensions caused by a loss of a Judeo-Christian ethos with discernment toward the skepticism secularization creates about the message of the gospel. This is a work of politically non-partisan, practical wisdom for thinking and living as dual citizens who honor Christ as Lord of all and interact with love toward those who have differing beliefs. Those in both pulpits and pews, and in parish and parachurch ministry, would do well to ponder these insights so that we might gain a much greater hearing in our public squares."

—**Eric C. Redmond**, professor of Bible, Moody Bible Institute, and associate pastor of preaching and teaching, Calvary Memorial Church, Oak Park, IL

"People are not the enemy but the goal of the Great Commission. But how do we carry out the Great Commission in a world that rejects our Christian worldview? In *Cultural Intelligence,* noted New Testament scholar Darrell Bock helps us understand how our divine imperative to love one another drives us to engage people who disagree with us. Moreover, he shows us how to take real-life situations through biblical and theological lenses as the means by which we can participate in significant dialogue. I highly recommend this book, as it seeks to create a path for Christians who desire to live out their theology in an ever-changing cultural landscape."

—**Ben Skaug**, senior pastor, Immanuel Baptist Church, Highland, CA, and adjunct professor, California Baptist University

"When someone writes from their life work, a simplicity after complexity emerges proving deep wisdom can come in small packages. *Cultural Intelligence* is a not a long read but is full of deep wisdom. It is right thinking with compassionate tone equipping the reader to speak truth with love. Darrell Bock is training us not to confront culture, but to transform culture through scriptural grounding and relational engagement."

—**Brad Smith**, president, Bakke Graduate University

"I spent 35 years at Christianity Today 'preaching' the gospel's message of beautiful orthodoxy, so you can imagine my excitement over this exceptional book by Dallas Seminary's Darrell Bock. Written for such a time as this—with vitriol characterizing our cultural speak and disrespect our motif for 'enlightened' engagement—Dr. Bock's *Cultural Intelligence* provides a biblically solid, intellectually accessible, powerfully practical guidebook for how every serious Christ-follower can live out impactful lives keynoted by gospel conviction and grace.

The world will only listen to the good news if we the church—as God's ambassadors—fully become the walking, talking expressions of his radical love. And to that end, Dr. Bock has written a primer for how our Spirit-directed words and opinions can be heard in the public square and ultimately make a difference for the whole of humankind.

Yes, this is an essential read for any Christian who longs to winsomely make Christ known in a confused twenty-first century where men and women are still searching—wittingly and unwittingly—for the one way, truth, and life."

—**Harold B. Smith**, president emeritus,
Christianity Today International

"Few biblical scholars and theologians have invested in and engaged with issues of culture as much as Darrell Bock. He offers sane, wise, and practical teaching to enable Christians to relate meaningfully and missionally with their often alien and fractured culture. This is a book the church needs and to which it should give attention to rethink its own identity and practice."

—**Klyne Snodgrass**, emeritus professor of New
Testament studies, North Park Theological Seminary,
and former president, Institute for Biblical Research

"Karl Barth has been credited with the well-known phrase, 'A preacher needs a newspaper in one hand and a Bible in the other.' What does it mean for church leaders and everyday believers to hold the Bible in one hand and a newspaper in the other? In other words, what does it look like to be biblically faithful while maintaining cultural relevance? Darrell Bock, in *Cultural Intelligence*, outlines for believers how culture and theology interact in the context of the church's mission. With Scripture as his guide, Bock masterfully articulates a way in which believers can gently and graciously navigate the tumultuous waters of cultural complexity while focusing on the church's core mission. This book couldn't come at a more appropriate time."

—**Ed Stetzer**, executive director, Billy Graham
Center and Billy Graham Chair of Church,
Mission, and Evangelism, Wheaton College

"Bock's pithy but robust word invites us into intelligent cultural engagement. We enter a gracious conversation and sacred space to discern how we engage our families, friends, colleagues and acquaintances, and by extension the world, to consider the winsome, radical Jesus and a coherent Christian worldview. In a society increasingly bereft of even a cultural memory of a biblical narrative, Bock invites us to communicate our faith from a refreshing 'life to the Bible' vis-à-vis the older model. I am helped to love my own secular city of Austin as well as the younger generations of my beloved Latin America where secularism has captured minds and hearts. Thank you, Darrell."

—**William D. Taylor**, president, TaylorGlobalConsult, and former executive director, the Mission Commission, World Evangelical Alliance

"As I read this wonderful and rich book, I was reminded of the sons of Issachar, who understood the times with knowledge of what Israel should do (1 Chr 12:32), a verse that has been my life verse for more than forty years. Reading this book reminds me of the story of the creation of the FedEx logo. We need to understand our culture and the forces that form it through relationships and engagement. Dr. Bock reminds us of the full purpose of salvation, the biblical imperative of love, and how we can understand that. Our cultural intelligence shows itself through the tone of our engagement and relationships within society."

—**Hon. Rollin A. Van Broekhoven**, federal judge, Armed Services Board of Contract Appeals, Washington, DC

"Not since the '60s has the American culture, and the American church, experienced so much distress and confusion on moral issues of the day. Not only are there constantly new issues causing highly politicized dissension in the world, but those disagreements have invaded the church walls as well. This has left Christians confused and divided; and has contributed to a growing disregard for Christianity in the public square.

This book by my friend Darrell Bock introduces many of the key issues culturally, biblically, and theologically that must be considered. It provides an excellent introduction to the complexities Christians encounter interacting with our non-Christian neighbors. And it seeks to provide direction for how believers can engage. Because of its length, *Cultural Intelligence* cannot treat these complex issues thoroughly, and the reader is left desiring more detail. But Dr. Bock's greatest contribution is the spirit of the book. As always, he seeks to move the reader to thought and actions that are guided by the commands of Scripture, and specifically the love of Christ."

— **Andy Wileman,** lead pastor, Grace
Bible Church, Dallas, TX

"At times of political crisis, racial tension, religious dissension, and much more, we need reminders of how to engage well with those around us tethered to the core tenets of our faith as a way to point people out of the brokenness and into the hope of Christ and his kingdom. Our public engagement is ultimately a fruit of our private discipleship, and this book is a much-welcomed resource that encourages and equips us to respond to others with graciousness, reason, compassion, mercy, and love. This book doesn't provide trite platitudes or easy answers but rather encourages us in the hard work of building relationships with others rooted in love. I'm grateful for Darrell's ongoing leadership in helping us develop a cultural intelligence that will help us transcend division, intolerance, and even apathy, and instead helps us pursue love of neighbor because of our love for God."

— **Jenny Yang,** vice president of advocacy
and policy, World Relief

CULTURAL INTELLIGENCE

CULTURAL INTELLIGENCE

LIVING FOR GOD
IN A DIVERSE,
PLURALISTIC WORLD

DARRELL L. BOCK

ACADEMIC
NASHVILLE, TENNESSEE

To the Hendricks Center team at Dallas Theological Seminary past and present. You are all special people, some still in Dallas and others now scattered after graduation into many countries of the world. Keep engaging with grace.

CONTENTS

ACKNOWLEDGMENTS

I have long desired to write this book. My team at the Hendricks Center has interacted with me on the themes discussed here over the past several years and have heard various versions of this material at an array of public events. So, to my entire team at the Hendricks Center, I offer my thanks.

Appreciation as well goes to Dallas Theological Seminary, for giving me the time and space to work on this subject. It is a rare school that allows research and study in an area that is not a specific curricular topic for a given class in the program. Dallas Seminary's commitment to cocurricular themes across the campus gave opportunity to explore this subject.

The relevance of this subject matter to evangelicalism has become particularly acute recently. I also thank the many churches, ministries, and Bible studies that have hosted my initial musings on these topics and given crucial feedback. The impact is on every page. These churches and groups were spread across the country, yet the consistent response I received was an encouragement to write this work. I have not peppered the text with footnotes, but I am presenting my own thoughts forged in these community conversations and discussions. Any faults in this manuscript are my own and do not belong to any of these organizations.

My wife, Sally, has had to donate much of our time together to give space for the travel and presentations represented in this material. Her share in this ministry comes in terms of sacrifice and support.

INTRODUCTION

We live in perplexing times. There is conflict in every corner of our globe—from Washington to London, Hong Kong, Iran, and everywhere in between. Besides all this tension in various places, our world has seen a huge set of cultural shifts in the past several decades. Those shifts touch on many areas of life. Among them have been seismic alterations in lifestyle choices that used to be taken for granted. Our own culture is not what it used to be. Through civil discourse (and sometimes public use of foul language), people debate marriage, sexuality, and choices regarding the preservation of life. Charges and changes are everywhere. The church, sensing a cultural war, has met this challenge and undertaken the battle. But has our strategy been right? Is it even biblically aligned?

Cultural intelligence requires that we understand what is happening around us and how to engage these changes well. To examine this need is the point of this book. Has the church's approach to doing battle been effectively defined and practiced? Have we missed the exact nature of the battle and misdirected our mission? We seek to answer those

1

questions and look again at how the church can engage in a biblically rooted way.

We proceed in six parts. First, we consider how we got where we are and examine the dislocation that the changes in our culture have produced (introduction). Next, we consider what Scripture says about engagement in the spaces and places where God has us (chapter 1), and then observe how Paul talked about culture versus how he spoke to it (chapter 2). In his life and words are major lessons in an intelligent approach to culture. Next, we discuss how to have difficult conversations with people who do not agree with how we see the world (chapter 3). We will also consider the things we do that prevent beneficial conversations as well as what we can do to have a chance at better cultural conversations. Then we look at the biblical call to love (chapter 4). Finally, we explore two ways to read Scripture and identify which one needs to become a regular part of our "Bible-to-life" teaching (chapter 5). To have an additional approach to reading the Bible can help us engage culture in balance with what Scripture shows as an effective way to live—and do so with respect to how God has made us.

The World Both Bigger and Smaller, More Complex

Our world has changed significantly in my lifetime, which spans back to the early 1950s. It has gotten simultaneously bigger and smaller. Given our vastly wider array of options now, our choices have become more complex, intensifying the pressure we feel. Cultural engagement has also become more of a challenge personally, but especially for the church.

From its first-century beginnings, the church was commanded to exemplify a countercultural way of life. In our American context, the culture war was launched in reaction to events in the 1960s and heightened in the 1970s. It is still with us, raging fiercely in all corners of our society.

Today's younger generations have not experienced the same degree of upheaval; rather, they were born into a rapidly changing world and have lived in the middle of it ever since. That one difference in their point of exposure has produced a separate set of sensitivities—sensitivities that are surfacing and adding to the tensions between the generations in the church.

How We Got Here

Virtually everyone recognizes that access to information has expanded, as have the options for making life choices that society no longer questions as it once did. So, what exactly happened, and what do those changes mean for the church?

Two innovations of the 1960s sculpted the challenging world we now occupy.

The first innovation, dating back to the summer of 1962, was the Telstar satellite. It provided the first live video link between the United States and Europe, bringing communication and information access to a new level. I remember my TV show being interrupted with "breaking news," and then I sat fascinated with the idea that a broadcast in one location could be affected by transmitting a signal into space from another location. Spaces and places were being changed.

Now flash forward to today. This kind of communication happens billions of times every day. No longer is satellite transmission the exclusive purview of big corporate networks. It is personal, and can be done from the palm of one's hand. Our big world is tightly linked, and we have been brought closer to one another than ever before.

As a result of this technology, we all became more aware of a wide world. It was harder to live in a protective bubble that crowded out most options. Such expanded connection and communication meant more people were aware of an array of options across their lives. Increased travel also opened up new vistas. Those who could not travel physically could do so digitally.

As perspectives grew, so did "perspectives as a matter for discussion." Our world became bigger and smaller all at once.

A second major innovation was the development and consequent availability of the Pill. This pharmaceutical invention changed relationships between the sexes. All of a sudden, sex could be had with little risk of pregnancy, minimal cost, and no personal investment. Where fear of pregnancy no longer reigned, freedom of choice became an option. An array of personal choices and alternative means of sexual expression became possible. Some of these choices existed before the Pill, but this drug altered the consequences, and millions opted in.

The result of such developments, and others like them, is that people have been exposed to more possibilities and have many more alternatives to choose from. In saying this, I am not evaluating those choices. I'm only observing the way information and options have intensified in our tightly connected, bigger-yet-smaller world.

Think of it: Who has not heard of or known someone who's lived with his or her future spouse before marriage or declared a same-sex preference? Who hasn't been in a debate about immigration, the cost of health care, the implications of Islam, or whether it is un-American to kneel during the National Anthem because of injustice? Where does one even begin to have conversations about such things with the hope of a positive outcome? How can we discuss topics like these without the conversations blowing up in our faces?

The Loss of the Judeo-Christian Net

Another factor producing all of this change is the removal of the Judeo-Christian net that once encircled much of Western culture. It existed a few generations ago to the degree that even if someone did not walk into a church or have exposure to Judeo-Christian teaching on a regular basis, he or she still understood its core values and, more often than not, gave those values some level of respect. Even if a person did not believe the Bible to be completely inspired (that is, divinely authored), it was considered a valuable source of wisdom about life.

There is no such net to catch people today as they "fall" into the life choices our culture makes available. In fact, things have changed so much that the church has had to wrestle with how to communicate to a decidedly distinct culture.

When the Judeo-Christian net existed, one could argue that something was true "because it is in the Bible," and people would treat the remark as worthy of consideration because the Bible was viewed as a reliable source. Now, the situation has changed so much that one needs to argue that something is in the Bible because it is *true*. That is a distinctly different kind of argument and, in many ways, a much harder argument to make.

Gone are the days where culturally one can use Scripture as an imprimatur for an idea's validity. Now one has to make the case that what is being presented fits an authentic and effective way of life.

The church is still learning how to engage in this way. Arguing this way is not to step away from Scripture, however. It means making the case for Scripture by explaining, "What God has said, he has inspired for good reason." Then the church has to spell out what that rationale is.

The reality of this change has rocked the church. Some Christians long for a return to the past in hopes of recovering what has been lost—a goal at the heart of the culture war many of us have fought for decades. However, Scripture has made it clear from the beginning that people of faith would always be a remnant within society and that to follow Jesus would mean experiencing pushback from the world (John 14:17; 15:18; 17). A disciple has always been warned to prepare for the reality of bearing a cross (Luke 9:23–25). Jesus spent the entire second half of his ministry making this clear to the Twelve, his original disciples, and nothing he said indicated that it would change until God fixes it all at the end of time. In other words, we have come out of an exceptional era that was probably never as good as we now remember it—and there is no going back anyway.

Still, none of these challenges or changes alters the need for the church to image God in the world. That is the assignment God gave those he calls to him. It is why the church bears the description "the body of Christ." We are called to be an incarnation of God's presence in the world, his audiovisual in a unique set of individuals and a special community. How we engage in showing God's grace and character matters. The content of what we believe matters, but so does our tone.

The church lives in a constant tension as it seeks to share the gospel, what is called the "good news." Sharing its message involves both challenge and hope. The challenge engages the way people live when they make choices independently from God. The hope-filled good news is that God offers a flourishing life to those who seek a relationship with him. As they accept his provision, they experience total forgiveness in Christ.

God intended for believing individuals, church communities, and the church as a whole to engage in a multilayered effort. Yet those of us in the West have tended to engage only at the individual level. We speak in very personal terms about our God. Many of our hymns are written in the first-person singular. Meanwhile, we could also be speaking about what a flourishing life means for our church community and how people can interact together as a God-honoring body whose standard of life stands distinct from the choices of the world.

The call for cultural adeptness has never been greater, nor has the need to view engagement far beyond individual concerns. So, what *theology of engagement* will lead us to interact culturally with skill and in line with God's call? How can we think about and live in the spaces and places God has us from day to day? How do we effectively engage the issues around us at individual, community, and even societal levels?

How This Primer Is Distinct: The Relational Layer

Most books on cultural engagement focus on either models of engagement, such as Richard Niebuhr's *Christ and*

Culture, or specific topics, such as *Faith in the Voting Booth,* the work by National Association of Evangelicals president Leith Anderson (with Galen Carey), or *A Practical Guide to Culture* by John Stonestreet. My own previous writing in this area, *How Would Jesus Vote?*, attempted something similar. And Andy Crouch's *Culture Making* took on the issue of contributing positively to culture and what helps form positive culture.

Such works are helpful, but this primer has a different purpose. We are considering how to approach all such questions with wisdom and skill by considering what Scripture says about engagement, as well as thinking about how culture and theology interact. We are asking especially what this looks like relationally, often when a believer's way of life is challenged in a conversation.

In particular, this primer considers our tone and the relational dimensions of such interaction. This is crucial because as culture and Scripture engage, we typically only think of the idea side of the topic without asking the subsequent questions: How do I actually interact with someone whose ideas are different from mine? How do I participate in difficult conversations? What does Scripture say about engaging those who do not share my faith?

There are six key biblical texts that discuss engagement. One of them is the most prominent "battle" text on this topic in the New Testament. What do these texts say about how to reflect our faith as we engage? How do they define our calling? One of the things we will see is that a misdirected and poorly defined mission is counterproductive to our call. Another thing we will see is that a targeted mission makes adept engagement—that is, cultural intelligence—possible, even when it includes a challenge to society.

As we begin, let me define *culture* and make an important observation. According to the *Oxford English Dictionary*, culture consists of "the customs, arts, social institutions, achievements, and values of a particular nation, people, or other social group." It is like the air we breathe. It surrounds us constantly. We interact with it always.

Now the observation: The singular word *culture* is a misnomer. What we experience are cultures, and their movement in relationship to one another is like plate tectonics. They rub against each other, sometimes resulting in disturbances. There certainly are tensions. This is life in a fallen world filled with options, some of them good, some of them bad, and some of them simply different. It takes intelligence and sensitivity to negotiate the combination of cultures and pluralisms we experience, especially as Christians. This book introduces how to think about engagement in a way that hopefully reflects Scripture, honors and images God, and loves our neighbor.

Finally, I am using *cultural intelligence* in a nontechnical way. The technical meaning is about how to understand culture with skill, how to be intelligent about culture(s). This book is more concerned with how to begin to get there, about cultural sensitivity, which sets the table for moving into developing cultural intelligence. It is a prolegomenon about engagement and how to get in a better position to live with the pluralism we all face. One cannot get to being intelligent about culture(s) without being willing to engage, listen, and many times, learn.

1

A Theology of Cultural Intelligence

Cultural intelligence requires knowing our calling as well as the real nature of our battle. The spiritual nature of the conflict means we must utilize both a spiritual perspective and divinely appointed resources. It also means appreciating what is going on with the people around us who have made different choices. In the section that follows, we will consider six of the most significant texts on the cultural places and spaces we find ourselves occupying, as well as how the resources we have enable us to engage wisely.

Six Key Texts

Ephesians 6:10–18

The key text is verse 12:

For our struggle is not against flesh and blood, but against the rulers, against the authorities, against the cosmic powers of this darkness, against evil, spiritual forces in the heavens.

Christians fight a battle in a fallen world. Scripture often speaks of the world as being opposed to the things of God and, as a result, opposed to believers. John 15:19 reads, "If you were of the world, the world would love you as its own. However, because you are not of the world, but I have chosen you out of it, the world hates you."

In a battle, it is essential to understand the calling and the mission. For decades the church fought a culture war where we often made other people the enemy. But this core biblical text on engagement reminds us that our real battle is spiritual. It requires spiritual resources, and we are armed with those in response to the conflict.

Ephesians 6:10–18 is the most explicit battle text among the New Testament letters. In fact, the Greek word for *battle* (or as verse 12 calls it, our "struggle") entails hand-to-hand combat, and the context involves arrows being shot during the struggle. It is a life-and-death fight.

Verse 12 of this text says we are in a wrestling match that needs armor. The metaphor is mixed, with arrows also coming from afar. In the passage, Paul is telling the Ephesians to stand strong as they resist the devil (vv. 11, 13). Ground has already been won. That ground is spiritual and is tied to things such as our theology and our character. That ground resides in the church and with the believing people of God. We need to hold our ground, not take over new territory.

This is what the text mentions as armor: truth, righteousness, the gospel of peace, faith, salvation, and God's Word.

Commentators debate whether this is about truth in the abstract or truth applied; whether it is about righteousness as justification or righteousness applied. Given what has been said in the letter of Ephesians to this point, it is probably all of this rather than either/or.

Both a guide to the battle and a description of the battle are present in this text. Strength is to come from the Lord (v. 10), and we are to equip ourselves with what he provides: his armor (v. 11).

If we were to state the key verse emphatically, it would read: "For our struggle is *not* against flesh and blood, but against the rulers, against the authorities, against the cosmic powers of this darkness, against evil, spiritual forces in the heavens" (v. 12). I emphasized "not" because on the other side of it is a fourfold description of the enemy that makes our opponent and the nature of the battle clear. Our mission is not to defeat or crush people. It is to stand with spiritual resources against an unseen enemy. These spiritual enemies are so invisible that people may not even realize they exist.

To repeat an essential point, the rest of the text names our resources: truth, righteousness, the gospel of peace, faith, salvation, the Word of God, and prayer (vv. 13–18). There is nothing about circumstances here. There is nothing about political ideologies here. The resources are our theology, our faith, and the quality and character of our lives as believers.

People are not the enemy. They are the goal. When Jesus sent forth his disciples with the Great Commission in Matt 28:18–20, he said to go into the world and make disciples. He did not say, "Go into the church and be disciples," or "Withdraw from public space." He sent the church into the public space, armed for battle with *spiritual* resources that only God and the gospel provide through Christ.

Now, let's think through our battle metaphor. We are members of the GIA (God's Intelligence Agency). Our assignment is to rescue people, as special forces do. We are to seek to rescue people from the clutches of unseen enemies. Those people walk "according to the ways of this world" (Eph 2:2)—a reality that should not surprise us. It is unrealistic to expect people who are not connected to God to live in ways he directs. This is why the gospel is so important in this struggle. The gospel equips people with ability and capability that they otherwise do not possess.

What does a member of the GIA do, and what is the mission? The mission is to so faithfully and relationally live out the truth of God that a way of rescue is made apparent. To so faithfully represent the truth of God that our lives and words demonstrate a flourishing, alternative way of life—his way of life.

Your mission, should you choose to accept it, is to rescue people out of the clutches of destructive spiritual forces so sinister that people may not realize they are in any kind of danger. This is an enormous part of the challenge. People are in extreme danger, yet they don't know it or see it. Understanding that our special-forces operation involves the rescue of people in harm due to sinister forces they often don't recognize totally changes *how* I engage. If I see the person across from me not as an enemy but as one who needs to be recovered, as lost and needing to be found, I will engage differently.

This is not mission impossible, and this tape will not self-destruct in five seconds. This is the call of God, where we possess the resources to fight the battle he describes in the way he prescribes. Those resources are contained in and deployed through the truth we live out day by day individually among our neighbors, as the body of Christ before the world, and as believers engaging the world in ways that are distinct from how the world engages.

In the culture-war approach, we have all too often grown misguided in the mission, making people the enemy. In that faulty execution of our assignment, we've not only failed to accomplish the call of making disciples, but we have actually damaged the church by robbing it of its good news. Our challenges to culture, which were intended to attract, have sometimes been expressed so hard and so heartlessly that the recipients have been repelled instead. This is especially the case when we do battle in the same ways the world battles, or when we neglect to live in contrast to the world. As soon as we shed the relational distinctives that are the church— the call to love our enemies and to live authentically with integrity and grace—we look like any other special-interest group. Then people will choose cultural options with their own special interests in mind.

The damage to the church's reputation and the cause of Christ is immense when the mission is as ill-defined as we've made it. Masses of our own young people look at how we older generations engage culturally, and they reply, "No, thank you!"

Our assignment is to engage in this spiritual battle using the spiritual resources we've been given so that, by the distinctive way we live and love, others will be drawn in. That distinctiveness is most evident when we love our enemies as

Jesus called us to do. It is not an easy assignment, which is why it requires spiritual resources to accomplish.

Many biblical texts point to the rich resources we possess. Ephesians 1:3 says we have been given every spiritual resource we need from heaven, and we can praise God for that. Second Peter 1:3–4a blesses the God and Father of our Lord Jesus Christ because, "according to his great mercy, he has given us a new birth into a living hope through the resurrection of Jesus Christ from the dead and into an inheritance that is unperishable." And as 1 John 4:4 says, "The one who is in you is greater than the one who is in the world." This is true no matter what the world says, does, or thinks.

Ephesians 1:21–22 likewise teaches that Jesus has been exalted over all other powers and appointed head of the church. Nothing can remove him from his place, regardless of what happens in the world. And nothing can alter our position in Christ as a result.

There is nothing to fear in the battle, for the spiritual resources we have are great and the identity we have is unshakable. Our assignment is to draw on those resources rather than rely on those that make us more like the world. We do so by engaging intelligently with people who think differently than we do. Not by despising or disrespecting them, but by seeing them as hostages in need of rescue. When we act like the world and perceive them as enemies, our rescue mission goes off course and we lose our spiritual advantage.

1 Peter 3:13–18

The key text is verses 15–16a:

> But in your hearts regard Christ the Lord as holy, ready at any
> time to give a defense to anyone who asks you for a reason for
> the hope that is in you. Yet do this with gentleness and respect.

First Peter is a great book. Much of it covers engagement.
The apostle Peter, the author, sat at Jesus's feet and took the
engagement class the Savior held as he prepared the disciples
to go into the world with the gospel.

One of my favorite engagement passages is 1 Pet 3:15, a
verse often used in Scripture-memory programs. We are to
be prepared to explain what we believe, our hope. Our faith
is not ultimately about ideas, though it certainly has those,
but is about hope.

Peter had one word he could choose to summarize
everything that faith comprises, and he chose "hope." That
hope is about understanding and appreciating why we are on
Earth and how we can connect to the Creator who made us.
First Peter 1:13 ends with the exhortation to "set your hope
completely on the grace to be brought to you at the revelation of Jesus Christ." We see that hope in the way that God
made the connection between us and him possible. It is why
the believer's message is called the good news. We get reconnected to the living God. We "get located" in the way we
were designed to live, both now and for eternity.

First Peter 3:15 is an exciting call and a wonderful verse.
But we often miss what is around it that helps answer our
question about what intelligent engagement involves.

Starting in verse 13, we're given a picture of the world as
it ought to be: "Who . . . will harm you if you are devoted
to what is good?" If we do good to others, things should go
well. Simple enough.

Only we live in an upside-down world, so the next verse reads, "But even if you should suffer for righteousness, you are blessed" (1 Peter 3:14a). Now, look at that verse. It anticipates that we will suffer for doing right, just as Jesus taught his disciples (Matt 5:10–12). It sounds as if Peter actually understood what Jesus had been saying in effect throughout the entire second half of his ministry: "If you follow me, there will be pushback. The disciple bears a cross daily. That is the world we engage in and with. Yet we are blessed, because our acceptance does not come from the world but from God and being faithful to him."

The next part of the verse is even more amazing. "But do not be terrified of them or be shaken" (1 Peter 3:14b NET). There is no cause for fear as we engage, even though we can anticipate rejection and injustice.

Now, I have to be honest. A lot of what I see in the church's response to our culture looks like fear or our being shaken. We fear for the loss of the Judeo-Christian net I mentioned earlier. We tremble at the way the world lives and the choices it makes, disturbed by the influences it produces. These are disturbing events, but they should not surprise us.

Our fearful responses never help us engage well. The believer's hope and identity rests in God. It is at this point that we connect to Christ as our hope and march into the world ready to engage, ready to give a defense, ready to stand firm, and armed with the spiritual resources that allow us to stand. And our dominant message is positive. It is about hope.

The tension of sharing the gospel and engaging with our culture is always a balance between the challenge the gospel presents to people about their sin and failure to live rightly and the gospel's invitation to enter into hope and a new kind of life. As we engage, we have to simultaneously challenge and invite. How do we do that well?

The church often fails by focusing so hard on the challenge that the hope gets lost. We so wish to highlight what is wrong in the world that we mute the hope that God has made available, or we defer that hope to the future alone. Yet his hope starts now, in this life. Now, the only reason to come to a new hope is because we realize shortcomings in this life, many of them our own. So, challenge has to be there somewhere. Yet our landing place is hope. It cannot go missing. Biblical hope is not about prosperity or a trouble-free life. It exists in a life that is plugged into God's purpose for creating us and aligned with his reasons for making us to begin with. So, in our engagement, it is important that we never lose the message of hope in the midst of a defense of the gospel and the challenge that comes with the gospel.

The only way for good news to be good news is for the good news to be in the message! And it needs to be communicated with an appreciation of why the news is good (because there is a rescue) and why grace is grace and not deserved or merited.

Often, we stop reading 1 Pet 3:15 right there at the mention of being prepared to give a defense for our hope. That is a major mistake. We don't merely offer our content, but the tone we present it with matters. Verse 16 says: "Do this [give this defense of hope] with gentleness and respect, keeping a clear conscience, so that when you are accused, those who disparage your good conduct in Christ will be put to shame."

Of all the things to digest here, let me make three quick points:

1. *Our engagement should come with gentleness and respect.* It is not to be delivered with fear, or anger, or resentment but with hope, because it is hope we share. We need not be threatened; we can be gentle and respectful because we know God stands with us. We engage, not arrogantly but humbly, because it is only by the grace of God that we stand in this hope. I see less of this gentleness combined with respect than I would hope to see from the church as it engages the world. We can do better here.

Gentleness and respect are crucial in engagement. The two terms refer to a positive kind of meekness and humility placed alongside a regard for those with whom we interact. Tone really matters because it communicates our love for those we challenge with the gospel.

2. *Our good behavior will be slandered.* This is the second time Peter has said our good will meet with bad. Every good deed will be punished. Do not be surprised when pushback comes. People don't like to be challenged, though it is a part of the gospel message. However, it's not the whole message. Hope still needs to be the dominant note.

3. *We are to maintain a good conscience while knowing God is fully aware of the wrong we have experienced.* First Peter 4:19 consoles us as we suffer: "Let those who suffer according to God's will entrust themselves to a faithful Creator while doing what is good." The shame our accusers

will have is before God. This is one of the reasons we need not fear as we engage.

In 3:17, Peter explains why we can conduct ourselves in this way: "For it is better to suffer for doing good [yet another mention of injustice!], if that should be God's will, than for doing evil." We are not to respond to the world in kind, even in the face of unjust responses. Disciples engage and show a different way of relating, even to those who reject them. This is part of how we love our enemies in a distinctive way.

The reason for this approach is what Peter says next: it is the example of Jesus himself (v. 18). He was the just One. He suffered and served in order to draw the unjust to God. Only note that the text does not only put it so generically. It says, "that he might bring you to God."

Peter personalizes it with a reminder about our own entry into grace. Christ is our model. We suffer because we are mirroring what he suffered so that we may be like him.

We ought to remember where we came from and how we arrived at such blessing. In other words, as we engage others and mirror Jesus, we need to recall that there was a time when God was gracious to us while our backs were turned on him. We should be able to understand what it means to be opposed to God and how God drew us graciously to him. That is the tone that matters.

We operate with cultural intelligence when we engage in the same manner that God interacted with us. We focus on hope even as we challenge people, and we do so with gentleness and respect because we remember our own experience of his grace.

Colossians 4:5–6

The key text is verses 5 and 6:

> Act wisely toward outsiders, making the most of the time. Let
> your speech always be gracious, seasoned with salt, so that you
> may know how you should answer each person.

Paul includes this brief but significant remark on engagement as he is offering final exhortations to the Colossians. Set in a context of prayer and the hope of open doors for the gospel (vv. 2–3), Paul turns our attention to how we can make the most of such opportunities.

Two terms are fundamental in this text: "always" and "gracious."

First, "always" is a technical term. The dictionary defines it as "all the time." No exceptions. That means twenty-four hours a day, seven days a week, fifty-two weeks out of the year, 365 days a year (and 366 days in leap years). There are no days off every four years — or ever. In other words, it is an emphatic time marker. "Always" is all the time.

Second, our tone always matters. "Gracious" is like the gentleness and respect we read about in 1 Peter 3. We should always be ready to share our hope, but always do it with this gracious tone. In fact, this is how gentleness and respect translate into application and action. It means to be gracious as we interact with those outside the faith.

The idea of salt as a preservative reinforces the imagery. Our speech should help things to settle — and to settle down. It should be constructive in dealing with issues, not destructive by engaging in personal insult.

Again, I'm not sure how well many in the church have been at applying this idea in their engagement, including many of our most prominent leaders. Yet how we relate what we believe matters. Without such gracious speech, we are not being culturally intelligent.

Galatians 6:10

The key text is verse 10:

> Therefore, as we have opportunity, let us work for the good of all, especially for those who belong to the household of the faith.

This short exhortation comes at the end of a long section where Paul has explained the law of love—the royal law that Jesus gave the church, the law of distinctive love. In Gal 5:14, he noted that the entire law is fulfilled in the exhortation to "love your neighbor as yourself." Once again, the relational dimension steps forward as the supreme application that God desires in our interaction with people.

Jesus had underscored in Luke 6 that this love is distinctive: it includes enemies and those who hate and oppress us (vv. 27–36). Jesus drove home the point that there is no distinctiveness when we only love those who love us; even sinners do that. The disciple is to do better, and the disciple's love should be greater.

Jesus told a story—the parable of the good Samaritan (Luke 10:25–37)—to make clear that our call is to be a neighbor, not worry about who is our neighbor. A scribe had asked him, "Who is my neighbor?" The question itself suggested that there are people who are not our neighbor, not our concern. Jesus's parable said, "No, that idea is false." Our call is to be a neighbor and to know that neighbors come in surprising packages, and Jesus underscored the point by presenting a hated Samaritan as the example.

So, in Gal 6:10, Paul ends his exposition on loving our neighbor with this: "Therefore, as we have opportunity, let us work for the good of all, especially for those who belong to the household of faith." This is a call for us to actually *do* good. Engagement is not left to words alone. We have to show through our actions what we declare.

A technical term in this verse is the word "all," which the dictionary defines as "any and every one." This love is directed toward all. It excludes no one. Just as Jesus illustrated in the parable, we are to be good neighbors to all.

With some texts, we are prone to get into a somewhat sinister debate about whether they apply just to those of the faith or to everyone. I think of Matthew 25 as an example. New Testament scholars have spilt much ink debating whether the text refers only to how believers are treated or how all people are treated. Frankly, it's not an easy choice contextually.

This text in Galatians suggests the debate may be somewhat superfluous, because all people are to be loved and treated the same. We undoubtedly ought to treat believers with kindness; then again, they are to be treated as everyone else is to be treated. When we say, "Believers are to be treated one way and others another way," we miss the point of this text. The call to love applies especially to those in God's community, but it also applies to all people.

The result of a too-narrow application is that we excuse ourselves from a responsibility we all possess and reduce our call to love all people. We also limit actions of love and care, undercutting the most powerful visual proof of our claims. We become like the scribe who asked Jesus, "Who is my neighbor?"—as if there is a limit to our care.

To narrow this kind of a text is to misapply the passage and fail at our calling and mission to love. I fear that in our recent past we have fallen into this trap. Cultural intelligence says our love is most distinctive when it includes all people.

2 Corinthians 5:17–21

The key text is verse 20:

> Therefore, we are ambassadors for Christ, since God is making his appeal through us. We plead on Christ's behalf: "Be reconciled to God."

Another major text for engagement is found as Paul discusses the gospel in 2 Corinthians 5. It is actually one of the most important Pauline texts in the New Testament. It gives a picture of our mission and how we ought to minister in light of the gospel.

Verse 17 reads, "Therefore, if anyone is in Christ, he is a new creation; the old has passed away, and see, the new has come!" This alludes to the newness of life gained at conversion, to one's spiritual rebirth. Specifically, it refers to being born again and the new life acquired by a connection to Christ in faith.

This verse explains why the gospel is at the center of mission and engagement: without the new life, living in ways that honor God is not possible.

There is a provision that comes with faith—an enablement that a person who does not know Christ lacks. This is because salvation is not just about forgiveness of sin but also about enablement for a new kind of life, a life that honors God and has access to the indwelling Spirit of God to live that way. This is what Rom 1:16 says is "the power of God for salvation." A formerly spiritually dead person is forgiven and made alive through faith in Christ. That person receives the enabling power of the indwelling Spirit of God to walk in God's ways. That is the message of Romans 1–8, and is what Paul calls being "a new creation" in Christ in 2 Corinthians.

Then Paul says this: "Everything is from God, who has reconciled us to himself through Christ and has given us the ministry of reconciliation" (2 Cor 5:18). And I sit here thinking that if I were to walk out on the street and ask someone, "In one word, how would you summarize what the gospel, or salvation, is all about?" and I just asked it open-ended like that, I imagine I'd get all kinds of answers: *Grace. Forgiveness. Hope. Salvation. Judgment.* I'm also willing to bet that if I walked into the average church and asked that question of people who ought to know the answer, the term *reconciliation* would be way down that list. It would not be in the top five; it might not even make the top ten. Yet Paul's one word to summarize what his ministry is about is *reconciliation*. Peter used the word *hope* in a similar way in 1 Peter 3, but in 2 Corinthians, the result of salvation is being focused on. God saves us to reconcile us to him and to others.

Now reconciliation is obviously aimed primarily at our relationship with God. When you read on in Paul's second letter to the Corinthians, he says more about this work of God: "In Christ, God was reconciling the world to himself, not counting their trespasses against them, and he has committed the message of reconciliation to us" (5:19). And then comes this wonderful verse, verse 20, that I think is actually one of the core verses regarding engagement in general. It reads, "Therefore, we are ambassadors for Christ."

Now, an ambassador represents a country. He also is a foreigner in a strange land. An ambassador's calling is to represent his home country and its values. He or she works for peace between the people the ambassador represents and the people among whom the embassy resides. All those things are in play. That is the picture Paul uses to describe what we do when we engage.

There are many parts here. First, an ambassador has a primary allegiance to the home he comes from, not to the foreign country where he lives. In our case, we are citizens of heaven and part of the multinational, multiethnic community God has formed around the world. Our home and representation are primarily with the people of God. In terms of priority, all civil connections come after these relationships. We represent God and his people first.

Second, an ambassador does not ask people to come to the embassy to get to know his country. He goes out and engages with the people of the land in which he now lives. The ambassador is out and about, learning whatever is necessary to understand the country where he or she resides.

Third, we are the bearers of a message from God. That message is proclaimed not only by what we say but by how we say it and by how we live.

These themes align with the previous texts we have examined. Christians are always ambassadors, visibly representing the One whom they serve back at home, that is, our heavenly home.

Verse 20 has even more to say: "God is making his appeal through us. We *plead* on Christ's behalf: 'Be reconciled to God.'" Do you hear the interesting tone of the verse that summarizes our message to the world? Once again, tone matters. The human-divine relationship is obviously the focus here. But what we offer is an invitation to be reconciled. It is a plea we give.

Now, the people we're pleading with are accountable to God for their response, but that also means their response is not part of my responsibility. The response is between that person and God, and so is the accountability for that response. The call within engagement is to be faithful in message and tone—to be a faithful representative of God, an ambassador who is worthy to be heard.

Reconciliation is an important theme in engagement, and to me, this category is the answer to the problem of life and finding our proper place in it. Without being reconciled to God, we cannot be fixed. Our human brokenness—and its estrangement from God—overshadows everything: politics, ideology, world circumstances.

Without a change of heart, only externals change significantly. We can posit all kinds of answers as to what might fix what's wrong in the world, but ultimately reconciliation is the divine answer to the problem that ails the human race.

Getting properly reconnected to God, and then letting his resources and his power and his enablement change how we act and interact—that is the answer. And in that process, a healthier dynamic can emerge, a better way of functioning in the world around us.

This is why the gospel is so central to our mission, and central in our engagement with culture. How we represent God in word and tone sets the stage for our credibility about the gospel. What we care about and how we care for others is part of building a bridge to the gospel.

Some people think the answer is in other places, especially in our politics. But we have seen that experiment fail. Israel had God as a legislator in the Old Testament, and they had laws he gave them, and yet their history was a mess. That is why God eventually said the solution is in a new covenant, where he would forgive them and put his law on their heart and give them his Spirit. Without a changed heart, laws and circumstances change little. So we need to be careful that politics does not become our answer for society's problem. Society's problem, as a spiritual issue, is deeper than any political ideology.

Verse 21 closes the section, "He made the one who did not know sin to be sin for us, so that in him we might become the righteousness of God." It is Christ who brings change.

In saying this, however, the message is not: *Engagement doesn't matter*, or *We should ignore the environment around us, including politics or other social concerns.* That is sometimes how an emphasis on the gospel is read. But that is a mistake. We show our care for people by engaging with their lives and what is going on inside them, being aware of what troubles them and why. We help people when we do not just argue but show them that there's a different way to live. One of the best ways to do that is to listen and care.

The reason injustice is so often a topic in the Prophets is because the prophets themselves cared about people, especially when people were being mistreated or marginalized. It is no accident that we have texts in Scripture such as Mic 6:8 or Jas 1:27 or 2:1–13. When we as humans, whether believers or not, appreciate what God cares about in relating to people, then how people — our "neighbors" — are treated becomes our concern.

Cultural intelligence calls us to see ourselves as ambassadors representing God, not so much as citizens of a particular earthly nation or political view, but as citizens of His kingdom. Our mission is to offer an invitation, pleading with any tribe and every nation to reconcile to God, showing love to any and all people.

2 Timothy 2:22–26

The key text is verses 24–26:

> The Lord's servant must not quarrel, but must be gentle to everyone, able to teach, and patient, instructing his opponents with gentleness. Perhaps God will grant them repentance leading them to the knowledge of the truth. Then they may come to their senses and escape the trap of the devil, who has taken them captive to do his will.

Our final text is hardly ever brought up in discussions about engagement, but it ties together several things the other texts say. The passage is a summary of Paul's advice to Timothy, a young pastor. It starts with Timothy's own character, which mirrors to a degree the spiritual attributes of Ephesians 6.

Here is verse 22: "Flee from youthful passions, and pursue righteousness, faith, love, and peace, along with those who call on the Lord from a pure heart." Righteousness, faith, and peace are part of the theological-relational attributes noted in the other epistles, especially in Eph 6:14–17. The content of this verse also overlaps with the fruit of the Spirit (Gal 5:22–23), attributes that are primarily relational as well.

Verse 23 argues against getting into controversies that lack substance: "But reject foolish and ignorant disputes, because you know that they breed quarrels." The Lord's servant is supposed to engage with a different set of goals: kindness, gentleness, and patience (v. 24). There will be conflict, but it takes a certain temperament to get through such tension well.

Two themes that we have seen before reappear here. The first is being kind toward all. Kindness is not selective. The second theme is gentleness (echoing 1 Pet 3:16 yet again).

Nothing about this is necessarily easy. Thus, it takes spiritual resources and maturity to develop such responses. It's all too common to want to snap back during a disagreement. Paul tells Timothy not to go there.

Perhaps the most amazing part of the exhortation comes next, in verses 25b–26. I repeat it because it is so significant: "Perhaps God will grant them repentance leading them to the knowledge of the truth. Then they may come to their senses and escape the trap of the devil, who has taken them captive to do his will."

There are several things of note here.

First, the person's response to God is tied to something God does. The ambassador is not responsible for the response of someone's heart. To come to repentance requires an eye-opening work of God. Still, in a battle of ideas or actions, we don't want to give someone cause for rejecting what we are saying. It may be unavoidable due to a difference of opinion, but we should never seek conflict. In fact, we should be careful not to descend into debate, but instead work to have a fruitful discussion. (We will say more about this later.)

Second, tone is again being highlighted, but we are only called to be faithful in sharing what we have experienced and what we understand by God's grace. Winning an argument is not a goal because it is not in our control anyway.

Third, the remark about escaping the devil's trap is another allusion to the spiritual battle of Eph 6:12. We now have come full circle to the fact that a person can be in the clutches of spiritual forces about which they are unaware. The members of the GIA are skilled at balancing challenge with hope.

Fourth, the result is a liberating escape. Rather than being trapped and captive, the person is given a different kind of freedom—one that links to God and his grace and fills him or her with enablement and hope. The result for that individual is a flourishing life and walk with the Creator.

Cultural intelligence avoids unnecessary disputes and engages in ways that are gentle. It also allows God to own the results of a conversation and trusts that by engaging faithfully and patiently, we are offering the non-believer an opportunity for a life-changing escape.

Conclusion

Engagement can lose its effectiveness when we lose sight of the primary objectives of our mission. A mission that is poorly defined or that incorrectly identifies what is most central can take us off a productive conversational path and may even result in real damage. The church's recent path may have unintentionally produced such damage because our mission has been misdirected. People are not the enemy but the goal.

In shifting times such as ours, we need a biblical agility that sees what is needed, alongside a relational ability to read and react. As we develop cultural intelligence, we gain this agility, guiding us to carefully listen and pursue gentleness while balancing challenge and hope. We also learn to appreciate the spiritual nature of the challenge of engagement and how to use those spiritual resources that allow us to stand. Skillful engagement means having a sense of our security in God so we do not fear no matter how grave the circumstances may look. Finally, cultural intelligence teaches us to understand that the gospel is the real answer for ultimate human transformation. Every other answer has severe limits.

Such engagement also grasps that not only is what we say important, but so is how we say it. Whether we think of ourselves as being engaged in the rescue of a lost person in danger or being an ambassador who represents the hope of God, the call is to humbly remember where we came from when God drew us to Himself. It was by the amazing grace of God that he stretched out a hand of invitation to us while we were being challenged about our need for God through the gospel.

Jesus's death for sin clears the way for the gift of life in the Spirit. The gospel takes people from challenge and deep need to hope. The result is a powerful reconciliation with God. Such reconciliation also opens up a unique kind of love for others that reflects who God is, what he did in Christ, and who his people should be.

None of this comes easy; it requires the fruit of the Spirit of God. Engaging properly with others requires an enablement and instincts that we do not have on our own. Engagement cuts against the grain and does not react as the world does. It requires a love that extends to all people at all times.

In the end, even if the world sometimes pushes back (as it did against the Savior), biblical engagement reveals the presence of God, who empowers us to live distinctively and speak to others with wisdom and skill. The result is a cultural intelligence that images God's character in our individual relationships, our church communities, and in our society. When we mirror him, we honor him.

2

Back to the Future: Lessons on Engagement from Paul

Sometimes it helps to know a little history. Let's look back to the first century, when the church was just getting started.

The church emerged from a small corner of the Greco-Roman world. It had no social or political power. All the cultural forces were arrayed against it. It was seen as fringe and treated as such. Yet somehow the early church was able to launch a movement that has far outlasted Rome, the world-encompassing power at the time. There may be lessons in intelligent engagement for us by going back to the future.

I want to explore two passages involving the apostle Paul and what I think they teach us about engaging culture. These passages are important because together they reflect a holistic perspective on what Paul said about engaging, as well as how he actually engaged. The two texts are Rom 1:18–32, where Paul describes his cultural context, and Acts 17:16–34, where he speaks to that very same culture.

So, how did Paul talk about culture, and then how did he engage it? Is there a difference between what Paul said about culture and the way he addressed it? Was there a tonal shift? If so, does that difference matter?

His tone about culture and how he engaged culture is what we are focused on. The difference in the two approaches is so great that more skeptical scholars argue "This cannot be the same person," and they question the account in Acts. However, by doing so, the opportunity for a real lesson about engagement is lost.

Such skepticism isn't justified once a person thinks through what is taking place. We are given important application about how to engage, especially in a culture that is functioning in ways that are so distinct from the perspectives of faith.

As background for thinking about these questions, consider this: Our world is changing, but in many ways we as a church community are going back to the future. In other words, our world is becoming more like the world that the earliest church lived in. So the way the early church engaged culture can teach us much about negotiating our own future.

Culturally, as we have already noted, we have shifted away from a personal knowledge of Scripture. It used to be that you could share the gospel and confidently assume that the people you were sharing with would have *at least* some basic knowledge of Scripture's teachings. But today we are encountering more and more people who know very little about the Bible at all. In fact, what they know about the faith is what the culture has said about it—and modern society's perception of our faith is not the best indication of what Christianity is about. Consequently, we often talk past each other because of misunderstanding.

In addition, for the first two centuries of America's existence, Judeo-Christian values served as a "net" beneath the culture, shaping how people thought about issues. Our national history, however, is the exception rather than the rule. In many places in the rest of the world and across time, Christianity has functioned as a minority culture. Yet even in America, this exceptional period of assumed Christian perspective and respect is now, for the most part, gone. Only in pockets of the South and the Midwest are such values still significantly present.

Given this scenario, where do we start in our task to engage culture? How do we work our way toward the calling of the Great Commission in this new, yet not-so-new culture? One solution is to look for models in the great ages of Christian faith, such as the Reformation or Puritan eras. Or we could adopt the methodologies of specific figures such as Abraham Kuyper, William Wilberforce, or Francis Schaeffer. However, all of these examples have only limited use for our context, for they occurred in a culture that was primarily undergirded by Judeo-Christian understanding. With that net gone, there is no longer any place to "land" culturally. The perspective of our audience has radically changed, leaving us much work to do if we want to communicate effectively. What was available to our predecessors as a landing place is far less available to us.

Because we cannot go back to that bygone era, there is a great advantage to focusing our perspective on the early Christian church's approach. Their culture was far more like ours today, in that it did not have a "net" of shared values. And Christianity did not have a social presence in places of societal power.

We need to go back to the future and sit again at Paul's feet and learn from the early church. We need to learn from them because not only does our situation resemble theirs, but their approach was particularly effective.

What can we learn from such a trip back in time?

The Core Tension of Engagement

To examine Paul's communication strategies, I will compare two passages: Rom 1:18–32 and Acts 17, which records his speech at Mars' Hill (or, the Areopagus).

I'll argue first that in Romans 1, we are privy to an "in-house" conversation where Paul is evaluating the culture for the church. He is very direct and straightforward when speaking with the "in group." Yet when Paul addresses culture directly in Acts 17, does he take the same approach in his communication? No.

In these two instances we see the fundamental tension that we, too, have to negotiate in engaging and representing the gospel. It's a tension that we already noted: *With our daily lives, how do we extend a hand of invitation while at the same time faithfully representing the challenge of the gospel?* The invitation is the ultimate goal, since in it is the solution for every lost soul. That invitation is also a journey into a new identity and the transformation that only God brings.

It's an invitation into a space that is missing in the outside world, a sacred space occupied by forgiven and Spirit-filled individuals forming a community that is conscious about being the people of God. It's an invitation to not only a personal relationship with God but a connected relationship with like-minded and Spirit-enabled people who are called to live distinct from the normal ways of the world.

Rather than seeking to take over space in the world—a space that Scripture tells us will remain until the return of Christ—we invite others to join a community and citizenry that is transnational. A citizenry that, through its presence both individually and collectively, interacts with and calls others to join in its mission to testify to and reflect God in a needy world. Our mission as God's people is not to grow the kingdom but to be the kingdom and draw people in the process. As our presence grows in and through the nature of this kingdom, so should our impact.

There are tensions as a result of our message and our presence that will never go away. The Christian message includes both a challenge and an invitation. Meanwhile, we must be in the world but not of the world. And we have a call to both confront and yet love.

An inherent danger is that we will forget the need to pursue both the invitation of the gospel as well as its confrontational demands. Some people are so good at the confrontation that the invitation is hard to find. Other people are so good at the invitation that the confrontation fades into the background, with the risk that transformation is no longer in view.

So how do we function effectively within these tensions and keep our core mission alive?

Paul's Theological Reflections on Culture: Romans 1:18–32

The key text is verses 24–32:

> Therefore God delivered them over in the desires of their hearts to sexual impurity, so that their bodies were degraded among themselves. They exchanged the truth of God for a lie, and worshiped and served what has been created instead of the Creator, who is praised forever. Amen.
>
> For this reason God delivered them over to disgraceful passions. Their women exchanged natural sexual relations for unnatural ones. The men in the same way also left natural relations with women and were inflamed in their lust for one another. Men committed shameless acts with men and received in their own persons the appropriate penalty of their error. And because they did not think it worthwhile to acknowledge God, God delivered them over to a corrupt mind so that they do what is not right. They are filled with all unrighteousness, evil, greed, and wickedness. They are full of envy, murder, quarrels, deceit, and malice. They are gossips, slanderers, God-haters, arrogant, proud, boastful, inventors of evil, disobedient to parents, senseless, untrustworthy, unloving, and unmerciful. Although they know God's just sentence—that those who practice such *things* deserve to die—they not only do *them*, but even applaud others who practice *them*.

In Romans 1, Paul is exceedingly clear about what he thinks of the surrounding, dominant culture. His discourse on the Greco-Roman culture begins with, "God's wrath is revealed from heaven against all godlessness and unrighteousness of people who by their unrighteousness suppress the truth, since what can be known about God is evident among them, because God has shown it to them. For his invisible attributes, that is, his eternal power and divine nature, have been clearly seen since the creation of the world, being understood through what he has made" (vv. 18–20a).

My son once lived in Montreux, Switzerland, which is on the Swiss Riviera on the edge of Lake Geneva. After one of my visits to see him, I sent a scenic picture over Facebook, and somebody commented: "How in the world can someone not believe in God when they look at this picture?"

Indeed, the Creator is evident, but so also are the demands to live rightly that his existence puts on us as creatures made by the Creator God.

Paul continues, "People are without excuse. For though they knew God, they did not glorify him as God or show gratitude. Instead, their thinking became worthless, and their senseless hearts were darkened. Claiming to be wise, they became fools and exchanged the glory of the immortal God for images resembling mortal man, birds, four-footed animals, and reptiles" (vv. 20b-23). The apostle then shares the key text we noted above and its three-time refrain: "God delivered them over . . ." (vv. 24, 26, 28). I read this and sometimes wonder to myself if Paul was watching our late-evening news. As much as things have changed in our world, much has remained similar to the way it was.

Admittedly, Paul's confrontation (and condemnation) of tendencies in the culture is not the most politically correct text. It is direct and pulls no punches. Going on, Paul accuses the ungodly of the moral crimes that culture's choices represented, and lists them specifically. The range of "crimes" (or sins) is staggering: unrighteousness; evil; greed; wickedness; envy; murder; quarrels; deceit; malice; gossip; slander; hating God; arrogance; pride; boastfulness; disobedience to parents; inventing evil; and being senseless, untrustworthy, unloving, and unmerciful.

Something in this list catches everyone at some point. It sets up a foundational statement: all people sin and fall short of the glory of God (Rom 3:23). The need for the gospel described here belongs to us all.

In a very pointed conclusion to his confrontation of the sinfulness of the culture, Paul wrote in Romans 1, "Although they know God's just sentence—that those who practice such *things* deserve to die—they not only do *them*, but even applaud others who practice *them*" (v. 32, emphasis added).

Sometimes grammar counts. This is one of those places. "Things" is not singular; it is plural.

The plural term is significant. Paul's condemnation in this passage extends beyond the middle portion of the passage that highlights sexual sins. While the dishonorable behaviors he cites there serve as effective examples of how dysfunctional things have become because of sin, we are meant to read the list as a whole, as a reflection of the remarks about idolatry that he made earlier. Detachment from God leads to these sins. No one escapes a need for him, and no one escapes blame or accountability. Anything in that list disqualifies a person from honoring God and makes him or her culpable for sin. The boat of the needy is full.

Unnatural sexual behaviors are but examples of an array of ways we worship the creature rather than the Creator. Besides the particular forms of sexuality condemned here are other types of sin, including gossip, arrogance, envy, and creating strife.

Paul is laying the groundwork for exposing why everyone needs the gospel, the new life, and the sacred space that God provides through Jesus Christ. The apostle's indictment of the "all" in Romans 3 follows an indictment of the Jewish world in Romans 2 and this indictment of the Gentile world in Romans 1. In chapter 2, Paul says that in spite of Jews having the law, they are guilty of similar types of violation. The problem is not one that belongs to any particular group. It is widespread. Everyone is rowing in the same leaking, at-risk boat. Everyone needs the gospel: from gossips to the proud, from the envious to those who practice sexual immorality in all its forms. Paul's condemnation of sin is comprehensive in scope.

The lesson is important for engagement. A text that the church often uses to condemn some people actually shows the need of the gospel for all. The challenge contains the reminder that we all need God's grace. In the challenge is the setup for the invitation, *if* we remember God's supply of grace for us while we were in sin. This reality presumes the need to be humble and gentle as we share. The only thing that elevates our status in life is the new life of the gospel, where God has supplied everything.

Paul's message here is broad, direct, and clear. The gospel challenges everyone who is alive that they need a restored relationship with God. If left to our own devices, we all fail to live up to the standard God has set for those made in his image. No one has the right to look down on another person in terms of their need.

So, cultural intelligence recognizes the state of our society apart from God. The need for him is vast, and it is humbling.

Paul's Methodology for Cultural Engagement: Acts 17:16–34

Some key verses are 16 and 22–23:

> While Paul was waiting for them in Athens, he was deeply dis-
> tressed when he saw that the city was full of idols. . . . Paul stood
> in the middle of the Aeropagus and said, "People of Athens! I
> see that you are extremely religious in every respect. For as I
> was passing through and observing the objects of your worship,
> I even found an altar on which was inscribed: 'To an Unknown
> God.' Therefore, what you worship in ignorance, this I proclaim
> to you."

With the Romans 1 "in-house" commentary by Paul
on the severity and scope of sin in place, we now can turn
our attention to how Paul engages that very same culture in
Athens in Acts 17.

We know full well from Romans 1 how he views the culture's acts and actions. As we move from theology to meth-
odology, we transition to Acts 17, where Luke recounts,
"While Paul was waiting for them in Athens, he was deeply
distressed when he saw that the city was full of idols" (v. 16).
This verse could be a summary of what we get in Romans 1.
The Greek meaning for the phrase "distressed" is closer to
"provoked," as Paul reacts with obvious anger to what he is
seeing. His blood pressure changed!

Emotionally, we are in the same place with him as we were
during his indictment of cultural sin in Romans 1. In Athens,
Paul was addressing the Jews and God-fearing Gentiles in
the synagogue and in the marketplaces. However, there were

also some Epicurean and Stoic philosophers conversing with him, and in their assessment of Paul, they remark, "What is this ignorant show-off trying to say?" (v. 18). The literal reference here is to a bird picking seed, indicating someone who lacks substance—who is going from this seed to that one, not staying in any one place long enough to really sense what is going on.

Here on Mars' Hill, Paul is introduced as almost a sidebar entertainer. He is not respected. They don't say, "It is our honor to have a key representative of a new religious movement that is stirring our world and to whom we should give our attention." He is merely a curiosity. And yet he walks right into that arena and speaks, not backing off from the opportunity amid a difficult, disrespectful crowd. He engages, even as they treat him as a less-than-serious conversation partner. He is faithful, respectful, and even gentle in how he starts.

Luke describes the scene in Acts: "Others replied, 'He seems to be a preacher of foreign deities'—because [Paul] was telling the good news about Jesus and the resurrection. They took him and brought him to the Areopagus, and said, 'May we learn about this new teaching you are presenting? Because what you say sounds strange to us, and we want to know what these things mean'" (vv. 18–19).

This frames what Paul is getting ready to do in verse 22. "Paul stood in the middle of the Areopagus and said 'People of Athens! I see that you are extremely religious in every respect." His statement includes a double entendre that we should not miss: to be "extremely religious" is also to be potentially superstitious. So, Paul's usage implies a critique, but it's one that can be used to build a bridge. Challenge and invitation are side by side.

This is an amazing opening statement. How can the judgmental, provocative Paul of Romans 1 even dare to speak in this way? They are "extremely religious!" As a child of the 1960s, I read Paul's words and wondered, *What have you been smoking, Paul?* This introduction is so surprising that some claim this can't really be Paul—that it is Luke putting words into Paul's mouth. Yet to view things this way means the lesson of what Paul is doing is lost.

The way he builds the bridge *intentionally* is not to come out with a full-court polemic against his audience's deeply held beliefs and insult them. Instead, Paul is communicating a level of respect for their pursuit of spirituality, and then he moves to correct it by giving them pause about something they believe. In effect he says, "I see you are very interested and engaged with spiritual concerns, so why don't we talk about that together?" He will attempt to correct them by building a bridge from where they are to where he wants to take them.

In fact, the ancients *were* very religious. Their world was filled with gods. Temples were on every corner dedicated to an array of gods. If you go to Pompeii today, you will see examples of the variety of temples. The Roman calendar was filled with 150 religious holidays a year. (That is one every three days.) Romans called Jews and Christians atheists because they only had one God! Aware of their religiosity, Paul walked through that open door and entered a conversation. He did so with respect and thoughtfulness as to what aspects of that culture could be a bridge.

Bridge-Building as Methodology

Constructing an evangelistic bridge, Paul says, "I see that you are extremely religious in every respect. For as I was passing around and observing the objects of your worship . . ." (v. 22). In effect, Paul is saying that these listeners have diligently pursued a type of spirituality, but there's a gap in their thinking that needs to be filled. He is confronting their belief, not with an aggressive frontal attack, but through observations that are designed to generate reflection, to give pause, starting with where they're coming from and working from there to raise questions for them to ponder.

Writer Greg Koukl does a lot of work in this area of engagement through what can be called *dialogical apologetics*, which he speaks of as putting a "stone" in someone's shoe.[1] It involves giving someone pause about where they are and raising questions that stick.

Do you see the difference between this approach and a direct frontal attack? Do you see the difference between Romans 1 and Acts 17? This is the same Paul who wrote Romans 1. He knows the theological significance of idolatry, yet the text in Acts proceeds this way: "I even found an altar on which was inscribed: 'To an Unknown God.' Therefore, what you worship in ignorance, this I proclaim to you" (v. 23). He will try to fill in the blanks as he starts from their own starting point.

---

[1] See Greg Koukl, *Tactics: A Game Plan for Discussing Your Christian Convictions*, 10th anniv. ed. (Grand Rapids: Zondervan, 2019), 46–51.

Rather than beginning where he is and asking them to engage with his beliefs in one big leap, Paul begins where they are and walks alongside them to where he is. Or, more specifically, he starts them on that path and leaves the results to God.

But Paul faces another dilemma in this setting. How do you share the biblical story with people who have never read a Bible? Where do you start with people who don't know the difference between Genesis and Malachi? In fact, they knew nothing about the contents of Scripture at all. How do you build *that* bridge? It's a key question, as this is the case in today's culture more and more. Many people know nothing about biblical content. Where does one start?

Importantly, Paul does not begin with citing biblical texts. In fact, nowhere in this speech does he explicitly cite the Bible! Instead, he tells the biblical story by starting with the most fundamental relationship anyone has: that of loved creation and beloved creatures with the Creator God. In a paraphrase of Genesis 1, Paul begins by saying that "the God who made the world and everything in it" (by the way, that includes you), the "Lord of heaven and earth—does not live in shrines made by hands. Neither is he served by human hands, as though he needed anything, since he himself gives life and breath and all things" (Acts 17:24–25).

Paul is not backing off, but rather, building a bridge toward his missional goal. At the same time, he is challenging what temples and idols can do. This is Paul's rock in the shoe. Paul essentially says, "I appreciate the fact that you have a spiritual quest going on; let's talk about what that spiritual quest ought to look like, based on the truth of God as Creator."

Luke's report of Paul's words continues: "From one man [God] has made every nationality to live over the whole earth and has determined their appointed times and the boundaries of where they live. He did this so that they might seek God, and perhaps they might reach out and find him, though he is not far from each one of us. For in him we live and move and have our being, as even some of your own poets have said, 'For we are also his offspring'" (vv. 26–28). To clinch his initial point, Paul still does not cite Scripture. He cites one of their own poets, which leads the audience farther along toward his specific objective. Paul tells the story of God's activity and builds bridges.

In the spirit of Paul's rhetorical approach, I often ask my students if they could cite contemporary cultural aspirations that align with biblical values. This might mean taking song lyrics that probe a desire in life that aligns with Scripture and developing that idea. It might mean discussing a movie that raises questions about the purpose of life, or pointing to a dilemma within a movie and discussing how an awareness of God might address the dilemma. Working with a shared cultural story can be the bridge to the divine story. Such moves reflect cultural intelligence.

Results of Conscientious Engagement

After Paul builds the bridge from culture to the gospel, he confronts his audience with the invitation of relationship with God through repentance, saying, "Therefore, having overlooked such times of ignorance, God now commands all people everywhere to repent, because he has set a day on which he is going to judge the world in righteousness, by the man he has appointed. He has provided proof of this to everyone by raising him from the dead" (Acts 17:30–31). Paul starts with the idea that we are creatures connected to a Creator God, made to relate to God, and he ends by asserting that we are accountable for how each of us manages that relationship. What better way to approach someone who knows nothing about the Bible than to start with how we are created by God and designed to be related to him!

One of the challenges we have in engagement today is that not everyone accepts the existence of a God to be related to. So, we may have more work to do here than Paul did in the transcendence-filled ancient world. Still, no one can get anywhere in the gospel without this beginning point. The prospect of a purpose in creation and a place for humans in the design of the world raises issues about the point and purpose of life—topics that are often good to probe as bridge builders. These themes can open doors to discussing the gospel and inviting others to be connected, or even reconnected, to the living Creator God.

When Paul mentions the resurrection from the dead, however, the Athenians go off track. They were new to the idea of resurrection. In fact, for the most part, Greco-Roman culture didn't believe in this kind of concept. People either held to the dead being quite dead, their life completely over, or they held to an immortality of the soul. A bodily resurrection was seen as a new, if not impossible, category.

"When they heard about the resurrection of the dead," writes Luke, "some began to ridicule [Paul], but others said, 'We'd like to hear from you again about this.' So Paul left their presence. However, some people joined him and believed, including Dionysius the Aeropagite, a woman named Damaris, and others with them" (vv. 32–34).

With that, the passage ends. Paul actually won some believers with this approach!

Sometimes people look at this passage and conclude that this experience was a failure, to which I respond, "Bah! Humbug!" Some of Paul's listeners came to Christ. Also, his approach here mirrors his approach earlier in Acts 14:15–17. This was a set Pauline strategy for how to address the culture: Build bridges. Give pause. Start where people are coming from. Challenge. Invite. And show respect throughout.

Paul did not make a mistake we often make, which is to speak to the culture without being sensitive to one's audience. Even in his challenge, an invitation is present, as is the offer of hope. The storyline of his message follows a positive crescendo.

It is important to notice that there's no hint of failure anywhere in the narrative. People were actually brought to faith. Some individuals joined Paul and believed, namely, "Dionysius . . . , Damaris . . . , and others with them." Luke names two specifically, but mentions that more than that came to faith.

Now, here is my key point. In Romans, we have an insider text speaking directly to the church about the sad state of the culture. To be sure, it's a very negative state, and what gets said is said quite candidly. Yet when Paul actually addresses that culture directly, he builds bridges. He communicates a level of respect and commonality. He tries to draw people out from where they are and point them in the direction he wants them to go. He understands his challenge is not just to engage people about their sinful culture and show how serious their condition is, but to invite this culture into faith, into a new, sacred space that is ultimately the answer they need. He is offering them *hope.*

The goal is not only to speak the truth but to say it with a spirit of love, in a tone that both invites and challenges. Paul shows us the balance, teaching us how to engage in our changing culture. We do it by building bridges to the truth with a tone of respect in the midst of challenge. That culturally intelligent approach leads to wise and skillful engagement that is culturally aware and relationally sensitive.

3

Difficult Conversations: How to Make Them Better

Engagement often involves a difficult conversation. Many times, we know before we start the conversation that we do not agree. At other times, disagreement springs up on us.

In our current context, these conversations often do not go well. The differences are so great, the perspectives so disparate, and the passion so high, that we soon find ourselves in a debate—or worse. Is such a result inevitable?

In this chapter, we will consider how conversations work, the goals of engaged exchanges, and which approaches sabotage a profitable conversation and which ones help. A key principle to all of this comes from Jas 1:19–20: "Everyone must be quick to hear, slow to speak and slow to anger, for man's anger does not accomplish God's righteousness."

The Nature of All Conversations

If this were *Sesame Street*, I'd say that the word for the day is *triphonics*. This term refers to something playing on three sound channels at once. That's what most conversations are—discussions operating on three levels simultaneously: facts, filters, and identity. (More on these shortly.) The triphonic nature of conversation is important to recognize because talk is the primary way we relate to others. Whether it be in marriage, business, politics, or theology, over Skype or Zoom, on social media, by phone, or in person, human conversation is a precious commodity. Conversations are a valuable means of relational commerce, either connecting us to people or alienating us from them. Understanding how conversations work and what can make them break down is an essential skill.

But how well do we understand the dynamics of conversations and how we short-circuit them, especially in contentious situations? That is where triphonics comes in. What can get us off track is thinking consciously about only one of those levels. When we're solely focused on what we're broadcasting to others, we can miss much of what may really be going on. So, let's take a step back and think through how our conversations actually work.

Triphonics Level 1: Facts. The first level is the one we tend to focus on, *the topic at hand*. This involves what we are discussing and our contribution to the topic. Like Jack Webb on the old TV show *Dragnet*, this is about the content of our conversations—"Just the facts, ma'am." Here is where we concentrate our attention, communicating what we see and why, often with a goal of persuading.

Our core goals at this level are making assertions, garnering evidence, and making the case. We are lawyers in a courtroom, persuading a jury with passion and truth as we see it. However, when we set up a discussion only in this way, the path is set for a debate instead of a conversation. Admittedly, in engagement there is often a case to be made, and the rationale for the position you take is crucial. Yet the relational dynamics underneath those positions are crucial too.

It is here that triphonics steps in. The three levels remind us there are other things going on in our conversations than just the facts and the topic being pursued. And there is more at stake in the conversation than winning an argument. Sometimes those other levels are the real drivers in the conversation—an important point not to miss.

Triphonics Level 2: Filters. The second level that is at work as we speak is *a combination of emotions, perceptions, and judgments.* This is where our conversations can get murky, because people are capable of looking at the same scenario and reading it so differently. When I speak about this around the country and need to illustrate the point, I simply say I can explain this level in one phrase: *CNN versus Fox News.* These channels look at the same information but process it very differently.

At this level we see a strange brew of emotions and perspectives that actually work to filter what we hear and how we arrange or, more importantly, prioritize the "facts." Sometimes we promote these elements to level 1 status in our discussion, certain that they belong to the core of the topic we are covering. But they may not always belong there. These perspectives and filters may need to be assessed on their own merits.

Often, due to their mix of emotional drivers and differing perceptions, discussions taking place here require not only advocacy but a willingness to listen for why the differences exist. A core goal in good conversations is understanding these differences and the reason they're there. That is different than assessing who is right or wrong or in what ways somebody is right or wrong. Still, we do confuse these two distinct categories and jump to assessing before understanding. And misunderstanding what is happening at this level typically halts conversational progress.

Being aware of our own emotions, perceptions, and judgments helps us in engagement conversations, especially difficult ones. Unfortunately, we often seek to mind-read the other person at this level, by speaking to their state of mind and motives, which we actually do not know, while ignoring our own internal state. This can not only short-circuit a good conversation, but it is especially problematic because we are not always good discerners of what someone else is thinking or why. We end up blaming the other person for the breakdown in communication, when what was going on within us had an impact too. So, we should be slow to go in a direction that attributes motive to another.

Being aware of this second level means that conversations need to drive toward some level of mutual understanding before moving into the hard work of assessing what is being discussed. We need to engage in slow thinking, not fast conclusions. That includes being aware of what is going on within us as we speak, and at what level things are happening.

Most discussions, however, immediately leap into assessment mode, with each side arguing for and digging in on their point of view. As exchanges take place, the participants are busy forming their rebuttals instead of listening to what is being said. In fact, being aware of this is a good, initial litmus test of whether we're actually listening or not. Am I forming a rebuttal while someone speaks, or am I able to repeat what they are saying in different words, so that they would agree, "Yes, you're hearing me."

When we're aware of this filter level and the difference between understanding and assessment, there is a good rule of thumb in all difficult conversations. It is the Great Commandment of initial engagement: *First, pursue mutual understanding; then move into assessment.* When you're pursuing understanding, questions are sometimes better than statements. And, as we've just mentioned, sometimes it is of value to pause and summarize what has been said to you, receiving the other person's affirmation that you got what they said, before forging ahead.

Understanding does not necessarily mean agreement. It simply means you have heard what someone else has said and why they said it.

The second part of this sequence is critical. Understanding the "why" creates a basis for seeing the origins of disagreement, and it may also supply a basis for empathy, helping us glimpse the reason for a person's differing concern or priority. This entire process of working hard to listen rather than rebutting communicates respect. You've taken the time and trouble to really understand someone else.

Typically, when we talk past each other, it is because we are in rebuttal mode and not seeking to really hear what is being said. To consciously hold the pursuit of mutual understanding as an initial goal of difficult conversation can help prevent the talking-past flaw in our engagement. The serious, joint pursuit of understanding may actually clarify where differences reside and why. Better understanding also helps when the conversation does turn to assessing what is going on topically and what is taking place relationally between the participants.

Triphonics Level 3: Identity. The third level is *how our identity and self-understanding are impacted* by what we are discussing. This is the deepest and trickiest level, but it is also always in play in conversations. *What is at stake for me in this conversation, and how I am seen as a result? How am I impacted in my soul by what is happening? How is this playing out? Am I looking bad or good?* These things often go unshared—if I'm aware of them at all—and yet they may be directing how I respond and why.

My example here is an exchange that happens fairly regularly between me and my wife. I'll be sitting at my computer, working, and she'll come in the room to engage with me about something. I try to multitask. She then says to me, "You're not listening to me." Now my instinctive reaction is to prove her wrong, so I repeat or accurately paraphrase what she just said. Annoyed, she'll tell me, "That drives me crazy!"

At the core of this exchange are two different things happening in each of us. I think she has just accused me of being a bad husband, so my instinct is to prove her wrong by showing her I did hear her words. She is feeling marginalized because my attention is not focused on what she's saying. I am distracted, and she knows it. By my distraction, I am saying to her that she's not important enough to be given my undivided attention. She wants my eyes and ears on her.

Now I have a choice. I can defend my self-understanding about my ability to hear her while I work; I can claim I am still being her husband who is listening. Or I can understand that what she is really after is for me to engage her more fully, not just "squeezing in" her words and hearing her on a surface level. It doesn't take a rocket scientist or a PhD in psychology to know which response is the better one relationally. These in-depth dynamics are constantly in play in our conversations, and particularly in key conversations, yet usually we don't think about this level of exchange.

Consider what happens as we engage in difficult topics especially. If you're like me, you're formulating responses in reaction to what is being said even as you're listening. Often those responses are in defense of your position. The one element that tends to be missing in this mode of conversation is curiosity and deep consideration about what is driving the other person to express themselves as they are.

Three voices (triphonics) are in play in us at different levels, and the deeper two levels can drown out our ability to listen and connect to the other person in the conversation. The decibels of our own concerns can create so much noise that they prevent us from making a real effort to understand someone else. The danger is reaching an impasse before we've really tried to earnestly engage.

What can help us in these difficult moments? First, when discussions become challenging, become more curious as to why the person thinks differently than you (without trying to predict where the other person's head is). Let them speak, and receive their responses as sincere—rooted in genuine concerns. Avoid dismissing what is being said by imputing a negative motive.

Second, pay attention to the three levels within your side of the conversation, but also seek to understand where the other person is coming from and why.

Third, be curious and ask questions, *not to defeat the other person but to move toward mutual understanding* about why you disagree or where the differences and tension points are.

Fourth, work to understand before assessing. There will be time for assessment down the road, and it is better pursued once everyone can agree on what the issues really are.

Fifth, learn to accurately paraphrase in the difficult moments in a way that assures your conversational partner, "I understand you." The key here is that he or she gets to make that call about whether they're being understood. You don't get to say, "I do understand you, even though you say I do not." This is also something you can ask someone to do for you. When you take this angle, you are communicating that a core goal of your conversation is to dialogue—to understand each other, not just see who is right.

What does paying attention to the triphonics of facts, filters, and identity do as we engage? And what does paying attention to the other person accomplish in a conversation? It communicates respect and allows for a better exchange and connection. It also builds the right kind of empathy along with constructing some mutual trust. Trust can particularly be important in contexts where your stances are not aligned and the going is hard.

When we're sensitized to how conversations really work, the true reasons for differences can surface in ways that both participants can recognize and grow from as they pursue better understanding between them. Once people realize that we care about and understand them, they open up more and are in a better position to hear what we have to say, including any challenge we might want to raise. This may also open us up to hearing things we need to hear. After all, none of us is omniscient. There is a humility and a gentleness to this way of engaging.

Difficult conversations don't have to be things to fight through; they may become moments where iron really does sharpen iron. Being aware of the triphonics of conversation may just be the anvil we need to turn difficult dialogue into revelation and learning. To pursue mutual understanding (not necessarily agreement) can be a realistic, initial goal in difficult conversations. In fact, it may be a quite important initial goal that produces better outcomes once we turn to assessing the conversation points.

What gets in the way of such worthy goals? What sabotages our conversations and causes them to degenerate?

In any conversation, there are only three movements that take place once the hard place of assessment is reached and relationships are at stake. You can push against or resist someone, escape to withdraw from them, or move toward them. What's important to recognize is that it's possible to move toward someone and yet disagree with them. I know that sounds contradictory, but that's what I'm doing when I respect them by making the effort to hear them. It is why James spoke about being quick to hear and slow to speak or be angry (Jas 1:19).

The subtle option among these three movements is withdrawal. We may think we're making peace when we're actually moving away from the person, and thereby suggesting that they do not matter. (Remember, identity is the most crucial relational level that drives conversations.) Some of the things we do in conversation to resist or to withdraw may initially feel good to us but, in reality, damage the relationship. These can be acts of relational sabotage even if we think they help make our factual case. They are important responses to identify.

Acts of Sabotage in Conversations

There are at least five things that can take a conversation down. If we're honest, we all use these sabotages. More importantly, they are the examples we see regularly in the public square. I suspect you could identify each of these on television news on any given night on any given channel. Sabotage is an equal-opportunity employer!

1) *The Quick Confession with a Pivot.* This is a "well, sort of" move that in fact dismisses the acknowledged point. Here, someone brings up something that is a problem for the view I hold. The response involves quickly acknowledging the problem (the "mini" confession) but then immediately pivoting and turning the shortcoming back on the other side. I call this the "yes, but your side is worse" response. When it's more subtle, it sounds like "yes, but this is what we really need to pay attention to." This reaction fails to really be helpful for two reasons. First, it refuses to focus on what might be contributing to the problem or issue from the end I support. It may even downplay my side's role, pretending that it is small when it may not be. Second, even though there's an issue on my side, the pivot ultimately disrespects the problem that has been raised and attempts to pin the majority of the blame elsewhere. That is not a move toward understanding

but blame. It puts assessment in a dominant and often premature place.

2) *The Exorcism.* This is the use of a label to kill an idea. Here we label in a word or two something as coming from this "bucket," play "Taps" over it, and put it to rest as not worthy of more comment. "Rest in Peace" gets written over the issue. Both sides do it. We label something as *liberal* or *conservative*, *fascist* or *racist*. I figuratively can see the hand going up, making an *L* or *C*, *F* or *R* in my conversational partner's face as I verbally label—and dismiss—the point being made. I might as well say, "Be gone! Come out of him or her!" (*Socialist* or *fundamentalist* might be another pair of labels on the spectrum.) By labeling the remark, I'm in effect avoiding the details and true merits of the issue being raised. Conversations rarely get advanced when this is one's ploy. Just think how frequently this conversational sabotage shows up in ads about another politician's viewpoint. "Exorcism" is a lazy attempt at engagement, and is often among the most destructive of tactics. It's a grenade into the goal of understanding. In fact, it is often verbal bullying.

3) *Assigning Motive.* Another tactic is to assign a motive, usually a negative one, to the position being presented. Frequently this is done to suggest insincerity or disingenuousness, with the goal of indicating that an idea has no merit because its intent is ill-willed. To know another person's will requires a prophetic gift that most of us lack. It also communicates a significant level of disrespect, suggesting that the real reason for something is not what's being presented. This is a tricky category because sometimes motives *are* mixed and not always spotless. However, to start here is to essentially raise questions about integrity that may not be legitimate.

This sabotage attacks at level 3 and typically produces defensiveness or a response in kind. The conversation stops.

4) *Thinking Poorly about Seeking Common Ground.* This is a subtle sabotage because it operates underground and is rarely expressed. It's the feeling or conviction that if I move toward someone and acknowledge a point, then that acknowledgment represents a defection from my view. Realistically, it may indicate that my commitment is less concerned with learning and growing and more intent on digging in. A move toward mutual understanding, however, is rarely a negative move. It sets the stage for a better discussion once assessments are ready to be undertaken. Much dysfunction is two-sided. Recognizing that is important if we want to have more profitable conversations.

5) *Tribalism.* Tribalism says I can never show weakness or acknowledge a shortcoming lest my side lose ground. And I can never give ground, not even a few inches. Tribalism is a clinging to power or advantage, but illegitimately, because a possible truth has been dismissed. This type of sabotage shuts off constructive self-criticism and growth and nearly assumes an omniscience that none of us possesses. Even positive self-criticism is treated as a sign of weakness or defection from my side. An important counterexample involves the prophets. One could say they were very pro-Israel. They loved and believed in the cause of the people of God. They were tribal in that sense, but they also were extremely self-critical. They were honest about when their side came up short. They recognized that growth only happens when shortcomings are faced and dealt with. When I get so tribal that I cannot see or even consider legitimate fault, I am setting myself up for failure

in engagement and real growth. So, the question becomes, what can work conversationally?

Acts That Advance Conversations

There are five things we can do to advance conversations. Applying these approaches can help to turn a debate into a more genuine conversation.

1) *Own our own junk.* The first thing we can do is acknowledge where we come up short, owning our shortcomings. Rather than confessing and pivoting, rather than being tribal, we come to serious grips with our contribution or our side's contribution to a problem. We actually engage that shortcoming and look to what can change, what should be done, or how to think another way about it. We fix or address what we are involved with that is part of the problem.

2) *Stick to issues.* Another positive step is to stick to the issue at hand and move through topics one at a time. Among the things a pivot is designed to do is to change the subject— to move to a discussion that favors your side. Rather than dealing with something that needs attention, you try to jump elsewhere. This can short-circuit real progress. Owning your junk and proceeding carefully toward mutual understanding means actually working through the list of issues one at a time as much as possible. This can be called slow thinking because you're working through issues in a reflective, manageable manner versus randomly jumping quickly from one thing to the next. A benefit of this conversation advancer is that we acknowledge space for our own growth in understanding. By doing so, we also create space for the other person to reciprocate.

3) *Be honest about our own concerns and convictions.* An honest conversation need not hide one's concerns and convictions. It does not require that we abandon what we think. We just give more thought to how to say what we believe. We are patient with a difficult process—slow to speak, quick to hear—direct but sensitive. We engage with an awareness of the relational level of the things we're saying and the relational impact of how we say them. The way to gain understanding is for each side to be clear about what they believe and why. But we want to be sure the rationale for what we believe is sound. Genuine engagement can help determine that by exposing where we might have blind spots or gaps in our knowledge. The only way to get there is to be honest with what we are thinking and why. Yet, as our earlier biblical study showed us, this needs to be done with gentleness and respect.

4) *Be honest about where we need to listen and learn.* Being teachable and open is also a virtue in such conversations, giving space to learn from what is being said. Partial knowledge that is believed to be comprehensive knowledge is dangerous. It closes us off to growth. Part of genuine humility is knowing one's limits and being willing to see them when another person points them out.

5) *Develop the ability to parse layers within a view.* Learning to recognize and face up to the strong and weak parts of our own arguments may be the most challenging aspect of difficult conversations. The things I contend for rest on varying layers of certitude. Some things that I hold to, I am absolutely confident about, while other beliefs are in the "more likely" or "only probable" categories. That change makes a difference in how tightly I cling to a view or conviction.

I often tell my students that they need a scale on which to rate their level of conviction. It runs like this:

- Level A is "I am virtually certain about something." (I joke that I'm so certain, I might be willing to argue with God about it.)
- Level B is "I am aware of disagreement here, but I'm reasonably confident that I am correct."
- Level C is "If we get to heaven and you turn out to be right, I honestly will not be surprised."
- Level D is "Let's both be honest and flip a coin, because neither of us knows."

This kind of scale can help me assess how strongly I should hold a conviction. It also allows for the possibility of me moving from one level to another in the midst of a conversation. In other words, growth and progress might come as we talk. I may not change my mind, but I could become more self-aware about how strongly I hold a view or should hold a view and why. In such cases, the conversation has been a benefit to my own understanding.

All of this self-reflection can be disturbing to those who are used to simply making up their minds and holding opinions. It may help to reflect on the different kinds of discussions we have in the public square. The "difference in kind" often results in a different kind of conversation, or at least holds the potential for such. This possibility of structuring differently the topics in our conversations raises the question: What distinct kinds of conversations do we often face in the public square?

Types of Issues

I think there are basically three types of issues in the public square. Intelligent engagement means being able to recognize what kind of conversation I possess. This helps me to see what is really at stake.

My examples here will be selective and evocative. Anyone could add to the sublist in each category. I am more interested in showing the core categories.

1) *Real Core Difference*. This initial category involves those cases where the nature of the issue is so great, there is little chance for any common ground. The views being taken—and their suppositions—are diametrically opposed; there is no real spectrum of ideas for thinking about the topic. Though they're few and far between, these cases do exist, and usually a great deal of passion is tied to such issues because so much is at stake. Consequently, these conversations become the most difficult to have.

The debates over same-sex marriage and abortion fit here: human freedom of choice in both spheres versus the view that both marriage and the point at which life begins are divinely defined. It's hard to find any common ground in discussions with such diverse starting points. The challenge is how to handle this chasm of difference relationally and in a shared social space. Believers will contend that, in the end, all people will be accountable for these choices before God one day. They also will argue that the character of our society is impacted by the choices people make regarding core issues, and that no core-issue act is a strictly private one. (This is why many people of faith view such choices as "not just a private matter.") There is little doubt this category is the hardest to negotiate well, because the differences in perspective are so great.

2) *All Agree, but "How?" Is the Question.* A second kind of issue is where people recognize the same goal but disagree on the best way to get there. The example here is racial reconciliation. If we were to take a Gallup poll on whether individuals should be in favor of racial reconciliation, the positive response would be an exceedingly high number. If we asked how best to make that happen, we might be given several dozen opinions. Because the goal is shared, these topics hold much potential for common ground. Still, there is often much work to be done to determine what combination of ideas might help us to get there. The potential for listening is usually much greater in this category than the previous one.

3) *Biblical Tension because of a Fallen World.* I'd suggest that this last category—where a set of human or biblical values are in tension because we live in a fallen world—is by far the more common one. It also is the trickiest, because it is where blind spots most easily occur. My examples here are health care and immigration.

Let me walk us through the immigration tension. On the one hand, a nation has the right to determine what kind of a nation it wants to be, fix its laws, expect them to be followed, and be concerned for the security and protection of its citizens. These kinds of concerns are legitimate and lead to a stable society. Creating the tension here is a host of biblical passages that discuss having concern for the foreigner, living a life of compassion, being sensitive to those at risk or the marginalized who are in that position through no fault of their own, and so on.

Other texts speak of the principle of forgiveness, which is at the core of what makes our faith Christian. In addition, there is the ethical and moral awareness that America's current situation was fueled by our approach to immigration—where we as a nation virtually supported the presence of newcomers for decades by encouraging people to live here and not enforcing our own laws.

Now, what often happens with such issues is that each political party picks one side of the concerns to highlight and virtually ignores the other side of the equation. The competing values are cherry picked by one side or the other. Such prioritization, as previously discussed, sabotages a conversation. In our all-or-nothing, cherry-picking debates, we rob ourselves of the discussion we perhaps most need: that of how to balance two sets of legitimate human concerns. We never reach recognition of legitimate competing values, a recognition that might allow us to work our way through our differences.

This kind of two-way conversation should not be a struggle in a democracy. It is not legitimate to simply say we need to follow the laws, since laws that do not work well or that might have flaws can always be reconsidered and improved. But our tribal, pick-and-choose, win-or-lose approach prevents us from even beginning to engage in the conversation that may be most needed and might even be most productive if each side would only hear and acknowledge the concern of the other.

Take the issue of health care. We argue that this is an individual liberty, not a governmental control issue. Is that completely correct? Is that all there is to it? Is this not an issue with layers to it, where what is humane is for people to be able to get core care to preserve life (since believers claim to be pro-life) without suffering financial ruin or being denied access? Still, the challenge is how best to pay for access to such care. We have to be able to afford the programs we implement. That is being societally responsible.

So once again, we have an array of factors to discuss—all of them legitimate—as we pursue understanding and transformation. Mutually recognizing that we are discussing values in tension with each other in a fallen world can help us have a better and more respectful conversation.

Please note how little I said about political ideology as we wrestle with human values in tension. Many of our public-square conversations work in the reverse, with our ideology dictating how we see and interact with others. Sadly, political ideals risk cutting us off from a different kind of discussion—one that will be challenging but that may also offer some fresh avenues to explore.

Some Closing Questions

When it comes to public-square issues, I love to have folks reflect on a simple checklist of questions as a way to think through the options. Here they are briefly:

1. What about the issues we face has me hopeful?
2. What about the issues we face has me concerned? (We could also place "why" questions with each of these first two queries.)
3. How can I/we make it better?
4. What do I/we need to better understand or hear? In other words, what do I need to learn about?

5. Am I hearing something from another perspective that I need to incorporate into my own perspective on the topic?

6. Can I parse the layers I'm seeing and hearing on any particular issue? Should my degree of conviction change as I recognize and reassess these layers and their relationship to each other? Do I weigh these layers relatively differently after having had this conversation? (This last question is a challenging one because it pushes us to avoid an all-too-human tendency to oversimplify complex issues and not face up to their complexity.)

Once I've explained the three kinds of issues we face and the need to parse them, I often hear people say, "This discussion is too complicated or too nuanced." My response is that we've become too accustomed to treating issues as if they were TV shows, where the problem should be solvable in thirty minutes with two commercial breaks. Many of the issues we face took a long time to develop and *are quite complex*. To plead simplicity is to avoid the slow thinking that challenging topics require. It is to engage in a lazy manner, not with intelligent engagement. Such long-festering issues are not easily solved. They need hammering out. They actually require difficult conversations. However, such conversations need to be entered into with intentionality. That means working hard not to sabotage and working hard to seek a place of mutual understanding, even if sometimes that means agreeing to disagree after the work is done.

The value of putting effort into difficult conversations is that we might just achieve a better understanding of each other. We might come to better appreciate why different conclusions are reached. We might place ourselves in a better position for a wiser, more mutually satisfying assessment. We might just teach one another and grow. We might do so without building walls that isolate us from each other, and we just might create enough space to produce a somewhat successful, negotiated conversation.

Those outcomes sure beat where we are right now. Negotiating difficult conversations well is a key part of possessing cultural intelligence.

4

What Is the Purpose of Salvation and the Biblical Imperative of Love?

For the Christian, a core question is, What is the purpose of salvation, and for what does it equip us? Many people claim that salvation is only about the forgiveness of sins and going to heaven. Yet salvation is about more than that. Forgiveness of sins is central to salvation but is more like a hub than the only goal.

One aspect of salvation is the restoration of a fallen creation. Salvation is designed to take us back to being all that God created us to be when he made us in His image. In other words, the Great Commission is intended to reconnect us to the creation mandate—why we were created in the first place. The fall of humanity and our inherent sin have blocked us from the fullness for which we were created.

Salvation reconnects us to that fullness and to the God who created us.

Salvation is not about gaining a place but about regaining a person and learning to live in ways that are pleasing to him. So, we will consider the creation mandate first, then take a look at the purpose of salvation. Finally, we will consider our response to being saved by grace through faith in Christ, and where this salvation is supposed to take us in life and in the public square.

The Creation Mandate, the Ethical Triangle, and a Call to Love

In thinking about what God asks of the people he created in his image, a word surfaces that I did not pay attention to as a serious theological idea until I was twenty years into teaching. That word is *stewardship*.

The creation mandate of Gen 1:26–28 is a call to subdue the earth. God tells Adam and Eve in Gen 1:28, "Be fruitful, multiply, fill the earth, and subdue it." The call is to manage well the environment in which God has placed us. This is to be done as a team—male and female are both made in the image of God—and involves many races as the story of Scripture unfolds. This assignment to manage the earth well is one every human is meant to contribute to as a part of life's call. In that mandate, we are called to reflect the image of God as we serve together. Put in other terms, this is a core call for every human being in any era.

Alongside that mandate is a core ethical call to manage carefully our relationships with God and with others. This is best seen in the Ten Commandments, which consists of two tablets: one dealing with how I relate to God, and the other dealing with how I might fail in treating others poorly. What Jesus calls the Great Commandment also has this twofold structure: "Love the Lord your God with all your heart, with all your soul, with all your mind, and with all your strength. . . . Love your neighbor as yourself" (Mark 12:30–31).

This management element forms part of the ethical foundation of Scripture. It places us in a kind of ethical triangle between God, oneself, and others. This idea is reinforced as salvation is announced by John the Baptist. In Luke 1:16–17, John's mission is defined. That text reads, "He will turn many of the people of Israel to the Lord their God. And he will go as forerunner before the Lord in the spirit and power of Elijah, to turn the hearts of the fathers back to their children and the disobedient to the wisdom of the just, to make ready for the Lord a people prepared for him" (NET).

This verse raises the question: What do a people prepared for salvation look like? The answer is, they are reconciled to God. That reconciliation with God leads to reconciliation with others in the affairs of life. Preparation for salvation is relationally rooted.

This idea of a "prepared for salvation" people is confirmed in another text, when the crowd engages with John the Baptist's call to repentance. In Luke 3:8–14, John issues a call to "produce fruit consistent with repentance," for the Lord's arrival is around the corner. The Greek verb here for the term "produce" is *poieō*. The crowd's response comes in three parts.

First the crowd asks, "What then should we do?" The verb for the term "do" is also *poieō*. They are asking directly for how to apply John's exhortation. John's response is, "The one who has two shirts must share with someone who has none, and the one who has food must do the same." What's interesting about his reply is that when we normally think of repentance, we think of how the idea relates to God. Yet John translated that worthy repentance into how we treat others. God is not directly present in his statement, but the ethical triangle is clearly in view, just as in Luke 1:16–17.

Next, a group of tax collectors asks, "Teacher, what should we do?" Again, the verb for "do" is *poieō*. The answer is, "Don't collect any more than what you have been authorized." God is not explicitly present in this response either. Yet again, the concern is translated into how I treat others in my vocation, in my life's affairs.

A third question follows from some soldiers: "What should we do?" Once more, the verb used is *poieō*. The reply is, "Don't take money from anyone by force or false accusation, and be satisfied with your wages." Though God is not directly present in this answer, how others are treated in political and social affairs is the point.

Luke's Gospel is describing how God and his messenger are preparing people for the arrival of salvation. It involves getting them to consider how to be properly aligned in their relationships with God and with others. To turn back to God is to return to relating well with others. The examples cited are turning fathers back to their children and turning the disobedient to the wisdom of the just. This is what a people prepared for God's salvation look like.

When the Great Commission calls us to make disciples, it is asking us to cultivate people who are learners about the ways of God. A disciple is a learner. Surely one of the things to learn is to keep the Great Commandment.

One could say that salvation reconnects the creation mandate to the Great Commission. In addition, because we receive the indwelling Spirit of God when we respond to the Commission's message, we can reflect the Great Commandment. When we honor the Great Commandment, we honor God and image him in the way we live.

The idea that salvation calls us to be like Christ is saying a similar thing. At the core of how we engage culturally and intelligently is how we reflect the image of God, honoring him. Salvation is about more than the cross. It is about a new life reconnected to God and reclaiming the stewardship to which he has called all humans. The gospel takes us into this space.

What Is Salvation For?

Perhaps the most famous salvation text in the Pauline letters is Eph 2:8–9. Many believers can quote it by heart: "For you are saved by grace through faith, and this is not from yourselves; it is God's gift—not from works, so that no one can boast."

We do not earn salvation with our works. Salvation is a gift of grace and has a design to it. Unfortunately, we often stop right there and do not go on to read the explanation for these verses. That explanation is introduced with the word "for" in Eph 2:10. Here is the whole verse: "For we are his workmanship, created in Christ Jesus for good works, which God prepared ahead of time for us to do." This is *why* we have been saved. Good works do not save us; they are what we are now equipped to do as a result of salvation.

Let's ask, "Why does God forgive our sins?" and think for a minute like an ancient Jew. There is clear logic to what

Paul is saying. In the Old Testament, an unclean person could not go to the temple to worship God. So he or she would engage in a sacrifice or a washing to become clean, and by this, the person was then free to go to the temple and worship God. The picture of salvation is similar. We are unclean before God because of sin. Once sin is forgiven, we are washed clean, which baptism portrays. Now that we have become a cleansed vessel, the Holy Spirit can indwell us and enable us to walk with God.

The forgiveness of sins in salvation clears the way for the Spirit of God to indwell us and give us life. With that new life comes an enablement to do the works that God called us to when he created us. This is what salvation is for, and Eph 2:10 says as much, as does the theological plotline of Romans 1–8. It is no accident that the theme verse of Romans (in 1:16) reads, "For I am not ashamed of the gospel, because it is the power of God for salvation to everyone who believes, first to the Jew, and also to the Greek."

Paul was excited about the gospel because it is about God's enablement, a power that allows us to walk in ways that please God by managing his creation together and serving those he has created. What we were powerless to do in Romans 1–3, we are able to do by the time we get to Romans 6–8, thanks to Christ's justification leading into sanctification. Romans 6:4 says it this way: "Therefore we were buried with him by baptism into death, in order that, just as Christ was raised from the dead by the glory of the Father, so we too may walk in newness of life."

Because of forgiveness, we are no longer tied to sin. Being forgiven, we can live a new life because God's Spirit is now working within us. We have become a cleansed vessel.

A verse we considered earlier—2 Cor 5:17—says that if anyone is in Christ, he or she is a new creation. In John 3, Jesus referred to it as being "born again" or "born of the Spirit." Salvation takes us back to the beginning and the creation mandate. It also takes us into the future with new capability to please God in our engagement with those around us.

Ephesians 2 does one final thing that takes us into the public space. Verses 11–22 stress what the first good work is: the reconciliation of Jew and Gentile. The first good work of salvation corporately is forming the church, a diverse community made up of those who have shared in this forgiveness. By its nature, the church models reconciliation. That reconciliation is between people of previously distinct backgrounds. The body of Christ is a picture of creation being restored. In its very design, the church bears witness to that work of corporate reconciliation.

The Purpose of Salvation and the Imperative of Love and Engagement

The salvation story of Ephesians 2 does not end with personal, private salvation. The church is on a quest for reconciliation. Salvation brings the reality and hope of reconciliation between former enemies. Ephesians 2:11–22 explains how Gentiles, who were without God and formerly far away, are now part of the people and temple of God, sanctified by what Christ has done. Jews also had been brought to God through Christ. Both together now have access to God.

Verses 17–18 say it this way, "[Jesus] came and proclaimed the good news of peace to you who were far away and peace to those who were near. For through him we both have access in one Spirit to the Father." In the church, we are to show how God has restored people. By this we show why people were created to begin with: to manage the world well while being in positive relationship with each other. Despite the previous ethnic and social differences between these factions, what Jesus has done in Christ makes this testimony possible.

Here in part is what salvation is for: to unite us in the Spirit so we can function alongside each other and then go on and manage our world and its relationships well. The gospel is key in all of this, but that gospel is meant to take us into a place that models what God is after, especially in how the community of God lives before God as a united people and in the world (John 17).

The call, as Gal 6:10 says it, is to do good to all people, especially those of the faith.

Summary and Three Key Words about Salvation and Engagement

In our survey of cultural intelligence, we have seen three key summary words for salvation.

First of all, 1 Peter 3 gave us the word *hope*. The defense that we give verbally and the way we live point to the hope we have in Christ. That hope rests in a restored relationship with God that never ends. Such a restored relationship honors God as it is rooted in his mercy and grace. Forgiveness of sin clears the path for that restored relationship and the enabled capability to live a renewed kind of life.

Second, Luke 1 and 3, 2 Corinthians 5, and Ephesians 2 show us that the result of that work and our ministry's message is *reconciliation*, a reconciliation with God and between people. By means of the Great Commission, that reconciliation takes us back to the creation mandate, a mandate that means engagement and justice are appropriate concerns for those who walk with God.

Finally, Rom 1:16 speaks of the *power/enablement* to reach that goal of reconciliation. This verse shows that a response to the gospel is a necessity to get there. It also shows that the good work the church does enters into all spheres. Intelligent engagement demonstrates what is possible and models what God makes possible. It draws people to that ultimate, reconciling hope in Christ.

Done intelligently, our engagement matters, as does our tone. Both things mirror a distinctive kind of love that reflects how Christ loved. It also points to the theme and priority of the gospel: the drawing of people back to God and to one another. That is our calling to engagement in a fractious world.

Our call to good works involves reconciliation. It involves the Great Commandment to love God fully, and our neighbor too. No one is excluded. That love is to extend even to enemies. Engaging with gentleness and meekness should take place all the time.

The good work we do is a distinctive good work—it's unlike the way the world engages. That distinctive testifies to the gospel's power and credibility.

Put it all together and you have a cultural intelligence that testifies to God's presence in our lives and to the work of the gospel. Through that enablement, we can be the people God calls us to be in whatever spaces and places he has us. A call of salvation is supposed to be about such reconciling work of love, because in part, that is what salvation is for.

5

Intelligent Cultural Engagement and the Bible: A Second Effective Way to Teach Scripture

In thinking about cultural engagement, church leaders also need to consider how we handle and present the teaching of Scripture in the public space. The Bible is central to the church and her message, pointing to how God worked through Jesus Christ and developing the story of God's program as well as the gospel. It reveals the relevance of theology to life. It shows the presence of God.

Yet there is a problem. As important as the Bible is to the church, for many on the outside, it is irrelevant; they see it as an old, out-of-date book. This is part of the reality of the spiritual battle that the church faces. It's also the result of having lost the Judeo-Christian net around much of Western culture. Worse than that, because people have been exposed to Christianity in the West, the gospel message is not a "new" thing as it is in several other parts of the world.

There is history attached to the church's reputation—some of it not so great. In my church history classes, as we've discussed the church in America, the Northeast region of the country has been referred to as the "burned over" district, meaning that many of its inhabitants were exposed to the church as it was in the seventeenth and eighteenth centuries and walked away. So how does one handle Scripture in an environment where people think they know what it says, and yet they don't know. What they've heard about the Bible is either mistaken, or they only know the bad and ugly of the church's involvement and not the good?

This is all the more a challenge as we seek to teach others to how to read the Bible and how to share the gospel with their unbelieving neighbors. This is not a Nike world where you "just do it." Teaching the Bible to leaders and to people was already difficult enough. Now it has become even more difficult, partly because of the brave new world we have entered into in the past several decades with the technological revolution and partly because of the globalization that is taking place in the midst of it all. So how should we think about the Bible and use it in this more challenging context? This chapter runs a little deeper than our previous chapters because the problem needs to be thoroughly appreciated in order for the solution to be effectively applied.

The Boomer generation has witnessed a significant cultural shift that has produced an even more desperate need for theological *and* life relevance in a world that "is not my father's Oldsmobile" (since Oldsmobiles aren't manufactured anymore!). When the world changes so much, we need to wrestle with what that change means for those of us whose job it is to communicate or share the message of an unchanging Word in a changing world.

Context does matter in determining what needs to be addressed in order to build a bridge for the message to have a chance of being heard.

Realities in Our Changing World

So how did we get here? *Secularization.* The increasing secularization of our world will not let us get away with what we've been doing. As we discussed early in this book, our world is both larger and smaller at the same time. However, another factor is that most of our culture, including many people in the church, have compartmentalized their lives into the secular and the sacred. Secularization in its rawest form has no room for the sacred at all. But there is an even subtler form of it that is very widespread: the belief that the sacred space ought to be a private space. It should not wander into public or into the public's consideration. Keeping God in a box is the result, if He is not excluded from consideration all together.

Thinking about and responding to this environment is not easy, for there is a sense in which the world, though filled with God's presence, is a less sacred space than the church. Ephesians 2:1–3 speaks of the prince of the power of the air at work in the world. Scripture presents the church as a real, corporate, sacred space—a temple—that is also scattered into the world through its people. Those people in turn invite others into this special, set-apart space where God is especially present and indwells people.

It is no accident that the church is called the body of Christ. We are not speaking of buildings and walls but about his people. This is why the invitation in the gospel is so significant in intelligent cultural engagement. People *are* being invited into a different kind of space than the one they are used to functioning in.

What also makes this confusing is that our own conception of kingdom growth has been flawed. We speak of "growing the kingdom" and of "penetrating the world," even of "conquering it" in some forms of teaching. Those images could not be more misleading about what we are called to as a church. Our calling is to invite people into sacred space—a space that operates in and penetrates the world but that does not "take it over."

The world and its pushback will be with us until Christ returns. Our call is to be a presence in the world's midst that offers an alternative way to live. This call invites people not only to take a look but to experience the distinctiveness. This means that how the church conducts itself as the church and its consistency in shining forth this new way of life represents its most important tasks in engagement. Of paramount importance is how the church lives and functions as a community—how it serves in the world to show this loving way of life with its distinct values.

Thinking about that is challenging enough. But here is yet another layer to consider. The concept is *glocalization*, the interconnectedness of the local and global. This reality is now a part of our world in intensified ways. As we've already noted, distance is not what it once was. Technology and our means of communication have changed even from when I went to seminary. Being overseas and listening to sports from another region of the world is no longer a function of Armed Forces Radio. I can watch nearly any major event in full, crisp color from anywhere if I'm willing to pay for it. Our culture's shift in access to information is the biggest since the time of the printing press. More than that, people are moving around in unprecedented numbers, creating pressures that we hear in all the debates about immigration in many countries.

Something should not be missed, however, in all the emotion this change stirs up: virtually nothing can prevent the penetration of the array of voices and options in our world. There is no going back to how things used to be. Living in the bubble of a monoculture isolated from the rest of society is not possible. What we're faced with is how to make choices, intelligent ones, in the midst of such change and options. It involves equipping people for the cards life is dealing us. We can try to run and hide, but then engagement becomes impossible. We are called to go into the world, not to run from it; to be in the world, not of it.

Glocalization and the Loss of a Common Local Culture

North America is changing. With glocalization, the world—the globe—has come to us. We not only see the world and its globalization, we experience it with neighbors who are different from our parents' neighbors.

My neighbors and what they believe are not what they used to be. My kids went to a high school at the turn of the millennium where far more languages were spoken than the three or four that were present in my high school. The number of worldviews they encountered from their "neighbors" was far more than what I was exposed to. This is one reason

that Millennials, Gen Xers, and Gen Zers respond so differently to issues and people than Boomers do. Simply citing
biblical warrant for things is no longer good enough in such
a mixed cultural context.

Yes, the Bible is true, but if people do not recognize that
truth, then our claim to have life (supported by the simple
citing of a text) falls on deaf ears. The elixir of Scripture
doesn't "take" as it once did when the audience knew and
appreciated the Bible to some degree. We used to be able to
say, "It's true because it's in the Bible," and be heard. And we
still should do this now and again, because what Scripture
offers is true. But we also need to say it another way with
the same goal in mind. We now have to say, "It's in the Bible
because it is true. God put it there because he was pointing to
how life should be lived."

We must realize as well that we make this claim in a
world where the idea of universal truth itself is debated, if
not denied altogether. That makes all of this even more of
a challenge. No wonder the Spirit has to be at work to get
beyond the fog of secularization and glocalization!

These cultural dynamics raise some fundamental questions regarding application. How do we best prepare for
this challenging new world? How do we read and apply the
Bible? An essential part of the short answer is that there's a
real premium on authenticity, integrity, and how the church
demonstrates what it values.

The First Way of Reading Scripture: From Bible to Life

The way many pastors and lay church leaders are taught to
read the Bible has much to do with the way we approach

biblical interpretation in our seminaries. Seminaries are rooted in a university model, born in old Europe with a Judeo-Christian backdrop and then impacted by the Enlightenment. In these institutions where many of our pastors learn to preach and teach the Bible to God's people, the primary focus is on knowledge, often abstracted, with a concentration on disputes about the text and its meaning. Such an approach also often zeroes in on the individual, not corporate concerns or society at large.

I have given my life to wrestling with textual meaning, interpretive options, and theological disputes, but this immersion has mostly been focused on "in-house" disputes, potentially leaving us unprepared for the larger world in which we live. In noting this, I am not saying that what we've done is wrong. It's truly necessary for the well-being of the church. I am asking instead whether our approach has been incomplete and even, at points, too insular.

This first way of reading Scripture, then, is what I call *reading from Bible to life*. It is focused on determining the meaning of passages in relation to their context within specific books. Key questions are what the words would have meant to the original audience and how the passage and the broader biblical book fits within the biblical canon as a whole. Application in this approach is driven by this primary task of determining the meaning of particular texts.

The danger in this, the danger I'm warning against, is that the Bible-to-life approach often fails to meet people where they are and fails to consider the questions they're asking or the tensions they're living with. Our teaching and sharing with this approach tells people what to believe before stopping to listen to what they're experiencing and why, or what they may already believe. If we're not careful, even when we share the Bible with good intentions, we'll miss the opportunity to show them how the Bible speaks powerfully to the questions they're asking. Thus we have to be careful to balance our biblical teaching, giving time to where most of life is lived.

What should we focus on as we teach, preach, and reflect the Bible's contents to a needy world? Scripture drives us to honor God by being deeply concerned about character, community, and mission to that needy world. We are called to serve the city, to work to see that it experiences peace and prosperity (Jer 29:7). We turn to God so that we are also better equipped to turn toward others. This assumes that corporate realities are a big deal: both what we believe and how we believe matters. They belong together. Truth *and* tone matter, sometimes quite equally. One without the other is like trying to fly with one wing. It will not work.

Applying Scripture in a way that engages with relevance for life requires wisdom in contextual engagement. It is dependent on the Spirit. He is the One who guides our way through a fallen world and its inherent tensions. That world will remain fallen until Christ returns; in the meantime, we are to call people to a different way of life rather than passively awaiting the Lord's return.

One way we can invite people into sacred space is to show that we care about them. Our love and concern is our calling card. We are called to preview, as a healthy, functioning community, what is to come. When our culture was substantially Judeo-Christian, the model of appealing simply to Scripture worked most of the time. Now there's a need to reflect and "incarnate" Scripture to a world that otherwise is unfamiliar with God's Word.

How can we do that if most of the spheres of life are excluded from that conversation? If we never let the sacred be seen, how can we invite someone into that space? Words alone are not enough. A loving church makes God's truth known by making it relationally visible.

Competing Worldviews in Open Access

Our traditional way of handling Scripture struggles to connect with unbelievers more than it once did. Globalization, greater cultural diversity, and the loss of a common cultural background have gotten in the way. We act as if we can go from Scripture to life with no static in between. However, there are multiple worldviews in play that challenge our presentation of Scripture. Some worldviews claim there is no God. Others claim there is no truth. Others argue that the truth is only what you determine it to be. Life offers a panorama of choices, and for most people, their life has become more isolated from spiritual values.

The challenge for pastors and all of us who want to utilize the Bible as we engage is that the vast array of common life situations has expanded: there are more broken families, views on sex and sexuality have changed, violence and terrorism and greed are on the rise, just to mention a few. No wonder we feel overwhelmed by the task of reading and sharing the Bible today. No wonder so many people are searching to find their location in life. There is a great deal of static in our world when it comes to hearing God's message.

The Challenges of Corporate Concerns: To Expand What We Address and the Core Tensions We Face

The world is at our door. It can overwhelm us or we can engage it intelligently. It is a world that is crowded, complicated, contentious, and captive.

The unchurched need to be affirmed for aspirations that reflect biblical values (however weakly). They also need to be respectfully confronted in the public space, where life is pursued in destructive ways. Ultimately, though, they need to be invited into sacred space, where we believe the solution is actually found.

As we already noted, challenge and invitation exist side by side as the church engages in mission. This combination of challenge *and* invitation is perhaps the core tension the church faces today as she preaches to a fallen world that Jesus desires to reconcile. If believers are going to get help with their lives and help others, then the relevance of theology must be addressed from the pulpit and in Bible studies. It cannot be abstract theology alone. It has to address not only our Sunday-morning lives as we gather as the church, but guide us in how to function in the larger world from Monday through Saturday. This is where God has us most of the time.

These settings and realities really do matter, because where mission withers, there is a lack of reflection about how to live where God has us most of the time. Thus we need to expand our reading and sharing of Scripture to explicitly include these settings and time frames. We need to move our interpreting and sharing into such spaces. This is especially the case for leaders in the church. Most of their training does not take them outside the issues of private spirituality, of serving in the church, of how we live at home, and issues tied to evangelism.

This menu is a capitulation to secularism, for look at how many places in life are excluded by these emphases: our work, our affiliations, our view of public issues, even how we engage those areas (tone). Consider those spheres of life where our engagement is underdeveloped: where we work *and how and why*; issues in the public sphere where much of corporate life takes place.

This public space is where human values are inevitably displayed relationally and where a visible contrast is possible with how the world tends to function. We have to think *more corporately* about how secular and sacred institutions function in the world, and even how differing cultures interact (yes, those niggly, actually not so little, corporate dimensions). Where we have tended to park our focus leaves big gaps in people's lives. One result is that the secular/sacred divide is unconsciously affirmed, undercutting a robust discipleship. Another consequence is that the Bible and faith seem irrelevant to vast areas of people's lives. How do we invite people to walk moment by moment with God through much of the week, if much of the week's activity is left out of our sermons and our Bible studies? When we treat Scripture this way, the secular gains the majority of people's time and space. No wonder the relevance of theology is often questioned and culture wields a large influence.

Where Do We Go from Here?

So, the questions are: how do I move beyond myself *in* the church, and how is the church to function *in* the world *for* the world? Christians, seminaries, and churches need to see this as their mission: to train leaders and guide people into a biblically rooted Christian life in all its spaces. This involves looking at ourselves both as individuals and as part of the various sacred and distinct public communities in which we live. We have to cope with a world that is pluralistic and glocal. We need to walk into and address public spaces with the right content and tone. We must consider how to understand Scripture, especially in daily choices, morally *and* relationally, conceptually *and* theologically. This has to include asking questions about those settings and times of day where most of life's choices are made.

Old Models Will Not Do the Whole Job Required

The models we have used in the past to achieve our mission ignore one crucial, game-changing fact. For example, the Kuyperian model, to which I am attracted and which was inspired by the life and theology of Dutch theologian Abraham Kuyper (1837–1920), did apply the Bible to all spheres of life in the late nineteenth and early twentieth centuries, to the point of impacting how some governments functioned. The Puritans who preceded Kuyper also had the advantage of a mostly Judeo-Christian backdrop. That backdrop is significantly diminished and often challenged today. It was like a societal safety net. The one game-changing fact is that this net is now mostly gone and cannot be assumed. Judeo-Christian values must be contended for and explained.

Our time is not like earlier periods, when Christian presuppositions, though declining in the culture, were still present, even if stripped of their theological elements. Today,

Christian assumptions have given way to a myriad of options, some of them not coherent at all and not trying to be. In these cases, most people have followed their cultural commitment to religious freedom so zealously that we as a people have little to nothing in common. As we noted earlier, our technology and global-supply chains are also making it much harder to achieve cultural coherence even if we wanted it.

Though our day and age does bear some resemblance to the early church period, the differences between our time and theirs are monumental. We need to appreciate how unprecedented our situation is. So, what does our response need to be?

A New Kind of Building

We have lost the foundations and cultural unity that used to be in play. Think of the difference between building on dry ground, on solid earth, versus building a structure that has to sit in the sea, like an oil rig. One has to hunt for the sea bed and construct rigging to get it to stand. There is more depth required to get there.

The study of Scripture and how we train people to apply theology to life needs to be calibrated similarly. The leaders we are training and the people we are preaching to come with less biblical background and a larger playing field than in the past. This is even more true of the people the church is called to serve. So, this is a desperate need. How should we deal with it? By balancing a pair of enormous tensions.

Two challenges demand our attention, especially in thinking about the corporate concerns we often bypass. One is the tension in mission between challenge and invitation

(2 Cor 5:17–21). The second is wrestling with the tension between the public space of culture and the sacred space of the kingdom.

Our invitation is tied to the deep-seated belief that the most important solution to life's problems is a personal relationship with God through Christ. This means acting with an awareness that real change cannot take place without internal, heart change. The combination of these tensions embedded in our approach to engagement requires us to do some fresh thinking about presenting the Bible, both its teaching and application.

A Second Way of Reading Scripture: From Life to the Bible

We need to switch-hit when it comes to how we read and teach Scripture. What I mean is, we have to be able to interpret the Bible in two directions while seeking and establishing the truth it offers. We need to go from the Scripture to life, as we often do, but we also need to work from the tensions and settings of life to mine the gold that is the inspired text. This is the second way: *from life to the Bible*.

In suggesting this second way of reading and handling Scripture, I am proposing that this way may have more potential today in our changed world than the traditional, Bible-to-life approach.

Today, some Christians still read from the Bible to life, but the reality is that most people read their Bibles in the reverse direction. They start with their lives, searching for answers to the dilemmas they're in, and then refer to the Bible. They are seeking specific help for the tensions they experience. They're sorting through their choices and seeking answers about what they should do.

For most believers, there *are* tensions that drive them back to the Bible. They are reading for wisdom and help. Reading from life to the Bible means understanding these tensions theologically and what drives them. It resembles the way case law works for a lawyer or clinical studies work for a psychiatrist. You start with a scenario and then break it down in terms of the law or the psyche.

To do this with Scripture in order to engage intelligently requires not just knowledge but relational ability. It involves not only individual piety but the ability to see things corporately, in the church and the world. It requires patience, sensitivity, and a comfort level with seeing the tensions that are there. It requires slow thinking and careful reflection. It means seeing the difference between public space shared with all, and sacred space that people choose to enter or are drawn by God to occupy.

Sacred space involves a distinctive space within the world of public space that God invites us to enter through faith in Christ. There, God equips us with his Spirit to participate in his work, giving us discernment and wisdom and other capabilities we formerly lacked. The sacred space exists in the midst of the larger public space and always faces the pressure public space puts on it. Distinguishing the two spaces and what is realistically possible in each is an important part of this discussion.

Beyond this public/sacred space strain, yet another tension faces us. It is tied to our mission and message. As believers, we have to cope with how the fallen world challenges and sometimes even shapes our view and experience of life.

The world often requires us to engage in ways that already challenge what we hold dear, even as we invite people into the distinctive experience the gospel brings.

Are you picking up a theme about the ongoing tensions of life that careful Bible reading must address? Awareness of life in tension is a core part of the interpretive approach for reading from life back to the Bible. *We have to identify those tensions, theologically assess them in their various dimensions, and balance them, not cherry-pick between them.* That is not always clear or easy. But it's important to have a theology that integrates divine values in life's array of settings; in the face of real, often uncompromising, tensions. This does not mean that we take someone's life or experience as authoritative for determining the meaning of Scripture, but it does mean recognizing that life is messy.

With humility we should consider whether we are limiting how widely Scripture can speak to life. We may need to recognize the depth of tension and the messiness of life and reassess those things biblically so that a better or clearer path can be found by sorting out all the elements at work. This will often involve challenging the beliefs and values of our culture, but it also may require some empathy to touch the person in their need. We need to recall that they are held in the grip of something they may not entirely sense or something that is overwhelming to them.

To be able to handle life and the Bible in a mostly secular context, and to show others how to bring the Bible into their work and their communities is cultural intelligence at work. We live in a real pluralism of beliefs. We face competing claims about the truth and ultimate reality every day. Yet we are still called to personal and collective faithfulness while living in a world which may well choose life paths and beliefs that are different than or even opposite of our own.

We also need to recognize the tensions of the spiritual war we are in, where the real enemy operates (Eph 6:12). Our call is to be an ambassador in that contentious world, engaged in a kind of rescue mission in a war where people are not the enemy but the goal (2 Cor 5:17–21). We have to learn to read, and help other believers read, the text and our lives in a way that does not cherry-pick from Scripture. We cannot allow the Bible to cancel itself out, leading to imbalance.

All of this involves a way of reading Scripture that puts it in direct and purposeful conversation with where we are. It is a *canonical* and *contextualized* reading. The space where God has me (and us) is a core part of that context.

It is *canonical* in the sense that Scripture possesses a theological unity across the entire canon, and we should always consider the part in light of the whole. Thus, we don't interpret particular passages as saying things that we don't see the entire Bible saying across its narrative. Our interpretation is built on expository, exegetical, and systematic approaches but ultimately relates to the whole of Scripture on a topic.

Our reading is also *contextual* in the sense that we're asking how Scripture speaks to a specific setting, paying attention to how our context may also have affected how we read Scripture, but letting Scripture have the final say. This way of reading is neither easy nor simple. It does not come fast, but it also reflects a mature handling of the full text and reinforces why knowing Scripture as a whole is a lifelong and important constant in the believer's life.

The Proposal

For years I have been sensing this partial disconnect between what the church is doing with Scripture and what is needed. Now you might be thinking, *Oh no, a proposal to change everything we do! That's nothing short of a nightmare. It will* never *work!*

I agree, that is a nightmare. It's also not what I'm arguing for in this proposal, so let me calm your nerves.

I'm not talking about completely changing how we handle Scripture. I'm speaking of the application we draw from Scripture and the ways we consider how Scripture speaks to our context. I'm talking about how we counsel our friends and neighbors, what goes into our teaching on discipleship and mission, the way we communicate Scripture from the pulpit or in Sunday school classes, and how we teach our children to study the Bible. What do we ask, how do we teach, and what questions do we pursue in the text? How do we handle Scripture, and what do we concentrate on as students interacting with the text?

I'm not proposing that we stop doing what we've been doing. I'm suggesting that there is another route we sometimes need to take that will equip us to better engage a changed context. On this other path, we are still delivering Scripture, and its teaching is still deep.

What I'm contending for is another lens or hermeneutical overlay through which we present the biblical material and connect with people and their lives. It's a proposal for showing how theological thinking and discipleship teaching are relevant. When the Bible is shown to be relevant, then respect for it is enhanced. When we show how theology matters, we also show to a secular world that God matters. And showing involves more than telling. It has to be displayed in our actions and tone. We have to live out what we teach. We have to show, not just know.

This is a great challenge because we often struggle as we move from the Bible to life, not to mention the reverse direction, from life to the Bible! If we allow this two-way lens to shape what we do from the start and see this end game of relevance as a crucial and necessary part of our goal, then through this dual approach to Scripture we can engage with life more deeply. We can prod people in the church to think in these terms and tones from the start. Maybe a new set of glasses with a fresh set of lenses will help us all see better, teach better, and connect more fully to life, giving us the recalibration we need.

Good News: Why Seminaries Are Necessary

Let me make one final point. I believe that seminaries are crucial to all of this. Some people think seminaries are not as relevant as they once were and not as connected to real life as they ought to be. But seminaries offer something that church-trained leadership cannot offer as easily or comprehensively. Residential theological education and good online structures give people access to a group of theologians with a broad level of expertise. Most churches cannot provide that in one place. That coherent, unified "groupthink" is still one of the most effective selling points for seminaries. Yet without relevance, people will be slow to appreciate the value of this benefit.

Groupthink that is siloed, or kept in isolation from the larger world (as is often the case with seminaries), will not get this done. The combination of silos and abstract, detached instruction plays into the hands of those who say we do not need seminaries. But genuine groupthink might be exactly what the church needs. An interdisciplinary environment, invigorated by this shared expertise and properly implemented, is necessary for the church to generate and sustain the kind of approach to Scripture that I'm proposing. It is an anti-silo approach, very integrative and synthetic—some of the most challenging work we can do. It needs a team of mutually engaged people with an array of expertise who respect each other. The possibility of online education, now made more accessible, also allows for this kind of training without requiring a person to fully uproot their life or leave their everyday ministry. Face-to-face teaching is best, but our online capabilities now offer potential for seminary instruction, which allows a better connection to a company of necessary disciplines. Such teaching can lead us into more effective ministry and church service.

The Approach

What exactly am I suggesting? Our common way of reading and interpreting the Bible is what I call *the Bible to life*. The ways of reading with this emphasis include working through a book; a topical study, a segment at a time; biographical work; and systematic theological reflection, with the Bible driving our theological application of Scripture. Such an approach is relatively neat and clean. The core theological ideas are in view; the ideal, or else the good or bad example, is set forth; and we look for principles along the way.

But what we need more of is a reversed reading, *life to the Bible*. This involves taking a specific, real-life situation or set of scenarios and biblically and theologically analyzing and formulating a biblical response.

Case studies dominate this approach, which is often more of an art than a science. *Life to the Bible* requires wisdom and discretion due to the varying tensions within the cases. Tensions are the natural result of life in a fallen world, and we must wrestle with how to balance those tensions in order to reach a biblically sound conclusion. Sometimes the choice is to determine the best among less-than-ideal options.

Two core elements are involved in working from life back to the Bible.

First, it may require a reorientation in how we present the Bible because we're seeking to shift to where others are in the larger culture. Do we teach something is true because it is in the Bible? Or is it in the Bible because it is true? The latter encourages probing and does not appeal to the Bible as the imprimatur of an idea. Although we as Christians esteem the Bible as God's Word, the people we address in the culture may not. We also may need to explain the relational rationale for what we believe. We are still explaining what the Bible is teaching but we are also suggesting why the Bible's teaching makes for a better way to live. In doing this, we are not neglecting the Bible, or its authority, or even its way of seeing things. We are simply noting that God tells us to conduct ourselves a certain way because it reflects a good way to live, the way things function best in the world he has created.

Even though it starts with a life situation, this is not theology "from below"—reading our experience and thoughts back up into what God has said—for we are still using the Bible as our authoritative lens for assessing the situation. We are simply working harder to understand the questions people are already asking and how they see the world as our basis for a better, more thorough assessment.

This all sounds pretty theoretical right now. The final sections of this chapter will give examples that flesh out what I mean.

Second, working from life to the Bible requires this understanding: arguing for something as true because it is in the Bible is not the same as recognizing that God has placed his teachings there because they are true.

Both points are valuable for us in application. Both approaches are rooted in what Scripture teaches, but the issue of sequence is reversed to help an unbelieving person (and perhaps ourselves as well) see that the authority of the Bible is tied not merely to its actual words but also more broadly to what it says about how God has designed life.

"Life to the Bible" requires more of the latter approach. It causes us to dig in and analyze why God takes us this direction through a particular text or situation. To get there, we often have to look at the whole of the Bible's teaching on a topic and not just a specific text.

In sum, "life to the Bible" means noting tensions and facing up to those tensions. It means taking life and its choices through the "fallen world" lens, working back toward how to be biblically righteous in the midst of such tensions. In particular, it requires balancing a constant issue regarding mission in the fallen world: How do I *challenge* my culture while at the same time *inviting* my culture into sacred space? How do I give pause to someone's thinking and suggest there is another way, a biblical way, to see life? How does that work concerning the topic I am studying? When do I confront? When do I invite? How and when do I mix them? And how do I respond when the options I face are not particularly clean?

For example, LGBTQQIA scenarios are loaded with such tensions. How do we define truth and pursue morality while showing compassion to those who are working toward godliness or who need to get there? Sometimes we must wrestle with how to balance truth and compassion, maintaining a hand stretched out in invitation.

How do we achieve that balance without abandoning truth? This balance is necessary because mission is an ultimate goal in engagement; because to embrace the gospel with its enabling power is the ultimate answer to all human need. Our solutions have to acknowledge and address the limits of what a person *can* do without the Spirit of God. This is where our politics, nationalism, racial identity, or ideology might get in the way of being missional. All these human answers have limits. If we're unaware of these tensions, we could mistakenly claim that more is possible in these spheres of public engagement than is realistic. To expect significant life or societal change apart from what the gospel supplies is asking too much of our efforts in these spheres, however well intended.

Life to the Bible reading involves more interpretive skills than *Bible to life* reading. This is not just about exegeting texts. Life to the Bible reading also involves synthesis— considering the scope of a text in light of other texts on that theme—and so it is more challenging. It works against cherry-picking among the tensions that are present within a topic. It asks how a passage fits in a wider way, given what the whole of Scripture teaches.

Such a wider reading recognizes that an isolated reading of a passage may distort or cancel out what other passages say about a topic. Failing to synthesize across the canon may tempt us to "force" the Bible to say things it doesn't actually say. Preempting the full process may prevent us from even seeing the problem. However, when done faithfully, fully engaging the canon, this kind of reading can be a powerful tool to see the array of angles by which Scripture addresses a topic.

We also have to be careful about drawing analogies from Scripture because the result may be to nullify the connecting text or a related, relevant text on the topic. It also means relating to people (not just ideas) and their background (often their culture and subculture) with an awareness of the social-cultural context(s) in which they function. This is not because those factors nullify truth, but because they may impact how people see their situation. That (mis)perception may need addressing when speaking to them about life.

There are numerous other elements that feed into how "life to the Bible" is done. For example:

1. *It requires reading our culture through scriptural eyes, looking both for positive longings and negative faults.* We tend to concentrate on negative traits, but there may be something to noting positive longings—the things people are hoping for that reveal the questions they're asking and their desires. These can build

bridges to the gospel and how it fulfills human needs and longings.

I find myself looking for glimpses of core life questions in songs and movies. When a prominent songwriter asks, "What's it all about, Alfie?" and turns to love as the answer, I want to say "Yes!" and then fill in the gap with more content—discussing what that kind of love looks like, and to whom and how it is to be directed. In Acts 17, Paul recognized a misguided spiritual pursuit, represented by the idol to the unknown God, then sought to redirect it. He was building bridges, starting conversations where the people had left off.

2. *It requires listening.* I call this getting a spiritual GPS reading. It means letting the person tell their spiritual-quest story or explain why they believe what they do. It can also mean initially surfacing past someone's issues, bad experiences, or false perspectives—the things that may color what we hear. Our tendency can be to correct people before we get the whole picture. As a result, we perhaps miss some factors to be aware of as we respond. We speak too soon versus being slow to speak. I tell people, "Put your theological tilt meter on mute at first, to hear just where the person is coming from and why. It may give you insight into how to engage down the road when the meter is turned back on."

3. *It can require theological translation.* Theological translation involves putting terms that we understand (but that someone else may not) into more mutually transparent language. As we engage, we have to avoid

in-house, "foreign" language. This involves thinking of synonyms or word pictures that explain what we mean. We use alternative terms initially until the concept is grasped. Translation work may also involve defining common terms in order to be sure my conversational partner and I are understanding each other. Sometimes our culture uses terms differently than the church does. Misunderstanding can be clarified in such cases. This is yet another reason to listen carefully first.

4. *It certainly requires a good biblical theology, drawing carefully on what the whole of Scripture teaches.* Theologically, life to the Bible involves a holistic approach that allows texts to speak from their unique angles and be placed together side by side to make up the whole. In other words, we consider how an array of texts on a given topic relate to each other, being careful not to let one set of texts annul or neutralize another set of texts that may reflect a distinct but significant topical angle.

This last point means we must be wary of generalizing application and moving too quickly into a broad, comprehensive conclusion. The issue may not be what is the constant or universalizing principle of any text (as we often teach students), but what in this specific circumstance triggers this response and why Scripture calls for something different in a similar scenario elsewhere. I think of the example from 1 Corinthians 8–10, where principles are given but the application shifts a few times as additional factors, such as location and context, change in the space of just a few verses (for example: meat in the marketplace, yes; in the pagan temple, no; at a meal, it depends).

Such a holistic reading across a topic requires nuancing in how we apply Scripture. We let the Bible's own seeming tensions and various topical angles speak individually and collectively. That means paying careful attention to all of these angles that Scripture gives, not removing some of them. We need to be slow and careful in our efforts to harmonize so that our result does not negate the depth and nuancing of the texts being considered, which may possess tensions that a quick harmonization may obscure or obliterate. Exposition alone can fail us here in our preaching. Interpreting specific texts or books alone will not achieve our objective. Unless one takes a full, careful look at a specific topic, exposition of a text may leave us nearsighted in our view of the topic as a whole. A solid contextual look at *each* passage will also protect us from the danger of prooftexting from one passage alone. (Prooftexting is the practice of using a single verse or passage, often out of context and based on personal bias, to support one's own argument on an issue.)

The Challenge

The challenge and call to action mean the church has to move beyond the university model of knowledge—the mere pursuit of facts—and learn a biblical integration of knowledge, relationship, and application that engages questions more directly. Such a shift has the potential to serve the church and society better than a strict, ideas-centered model. Moving beyond ideas alone to their connection to "life as we find it" includes challenge for change as well as the offer of hope for a better way. It steps into the array of life spaces that exist. To do this, we will need to give more attention to the methods and approach I am describing. It requires directly addressing more of life as it is being lived.

The hope is that structured teaching in this two-way approach will utilize both tracks and will better equip churchgoers and ministers for their task. This will pave the way for more effective leadership and teaching in the church as well. Our challenge as a believing community is to show how we can do a better job of applying theology to real life. To get there, we have to go from the Bible to life but also work back from all of life to the Bible. That expanded capability is another crucial part of having cultural intelligence.

Some Specific Examples of "Life to the Bible"

Let's take a look at some specific examples to clarify what I am and am not saying.

The kind of approach I'm speaking of is canonical and contextual. We're taught often to pay attention to the specific context of a passage. However, where a text fits in light of the teaching of the entire biblical canon is important to consider as well.

The canonical requirement is necessary because of how the Bible works, as well as the kinds of issues life throws at us. Many texts in Scripture operate in a specific context. Likewise, the answer to the ethical questions life raises may be impacted by the kind of context I'm addressing.

Another factor or layer at the canonical level is that as you bring many different passages to bear on a topic or theme, those collective passages may bring tensions that reveal important qualifications to be made regarding ethical principles on that topic. At the least, this has to be considered when asking how all of Scripture works together. For example, we are generally told to obey religious or governing authority, yet there are some texts that show disobedience to such authority—such as how Daniel handled certain situations or how Peter refused when the religious leaders told him to stop preaching about Jesus. These instances point to a limit on such a general principle.

A careful canonical study will examine what kinds of contexts are present when the exception applies. Only after we have considered such texts are we ready to speak to current life settings and examine whether or not they apply.

The three types of public-square issues I noted earlier are also a factor here. Allow me to review them to show how they fit into this biblical reflection conversation.

In writing *How Would Jesus Vote?* it became clear to me that most public-square issues divide into three categories. Category 1 involves real worldview conflict, where there is strict disagreement with little to no middle ground. Debates on same-sex marriage or abortion fit here. The ethical ground with which each side of this debate approaches the question is so distinct that discussion is particularly difficult.

Category 2 is where there is agreement on what needs to be done, but no one is quite sure how to get there. This is usually triggered by a different kind of experience in the background that raises distinct sets of concerns and sensitivities. The pursuit of racial reconciliation falls here.

Category 3 involves biblical points in tension. We live in a fallen world, and life is messy. What's in view here is where biblical values come into tension with each other and

need to be balanced. They need to be related to each other—
studiously connected, not merely chosen between—as we
seek to address an issue with balance. Most corporate issues
we face fall into this category.

The danger is that we focus on one biblical value and risk
negating the other. We cherry-pick and end up with a potential imbalance in the process. To recognize this tendency
means there's a lot of room for discussion on these topics.
Looking for and identifying the tensions precisely is key to
this kind of a reading. To miss or pretend one tension does
not exist will skew the assessment.

A common problem in our public discourse is that
we treat category 3 discussions as if they were category 1.
This can blind us to seeing if there is some kind of common
ground possible. When one biblical value negates a legitimate
concern, a full biblical perspective is muted and the solution
is not what it could be.

Why do most of our societal conversations belong in the
third category? A part of the answer is a fallen world, which
means tensions inevitably exist and have to be negotiated.
The whole of the Bible reflects that reality as it engages with
life. The challenge is that specific passages often give us one
glimpse of a topic, but that is not enough. These kinds of
usually large themes require canonical balance. The solution
is to recognize the tension(s) and go to work. Let me run
through some examples.

Examples

In this final section we consider examples from all the categories but will concentrate on category 3 because category 3

issues are often placed into category 1, elevating their importance. This move obscures the clarity with which these issues
could be handled. When category 3 issues are dropped into
category 1, they are usually oversimplified, and a discussion
worth having might be missed as a result. I save category 1
topics for last.

Racial Reconciliation. Here is a category 2 topic. We
know that Scripture urges us to be reconciled, both to God
and to each other. The problems in this area have to do with
appreciating the experience of majority-minority relationships and what those dynamics produce. I've done many
interviews on this topic on my podcast for Dallas Seminary,
called *The Table.* We discuss issues of God and culture there,
including this one.

For this subject I've included believers of various ethnici-
ties, and we have heard about their experience in American
culture. Those discussions have revealed how the experiences
of some groups are so different from my own. Things they
regularly deal with are things I have not experienced or, if I
did, I was in a context (another country, for example) where
I did not share the majority culture and the language. My
foreign-travel experience has helped me understand some of
what these fellow believers often face, although I can never
completely understand what it's like to be a minority dealing
with constant stereotypes.

Here the church's responsibility is to help people apply
texts on love, justice, and caring for those on the fringe
whose voices should be heard. Developing sensitivity to
these dynamics is a call of many texts (Isa 29:17–20; Mic
6:8; Jas 1:26–27; 2:1–13). The question is not where the text
seeks to take us, on which we agree, but how practically to

get there. In this category, a key commitment is to listen and sort through the options. This is usually not as difficult as a discussion in the other categories because the desired result is held in common. All agree on the shared goal. The discussion becomes difficult when we cease to be good listeners and fail to appreciate the distinct experiences that some have had.

Wealth and Money. Here is a category 3 issue. The accumulation of resources and wealth is something that is of value. It is tied to wisdom themes in Proverbs (10:15; 15:6; 28:8). Resources and wealth are part of the way we steward the creation and care for our families. Yet there is a danger lurking within this topic. Numerous texts, especially from Jesus in the Gospel of Luke, point to how the love of money can be a danger and distraction for people, affecting how they treat others (Luke 6:24–26; 12:15–20; 16:13). The prophets also spent much time challenging those who used their wealth in destructive ways (Jer 17:11; Ezek 7:11).

Here is a classic example of tension: something with good potential can be turned into something bad. In biblical terms, wealth is something to be handled as a matter of stewardship. Our concern for others is a way to balance this tension. But someone might miss this tension if he or she reads texts in Proverbs alone. We also will miss the other part of the equation if we only deal with certain texts from Jesus or Paul. We can fall into a kind of trap about class rather than use and responsibility. We might miss the instruction to encourage generosity and compassion on the one hand for those who have, and being responsible with resources on the other hand for those who lack.

How do we bring balance to these life tensions in our observations and teaching about wealth, resources, and poverty? Along with personal responsibility, do we wrestle with structural questions since we are speaking of politics and cultural realities? Do we recognize how these considerations can impact the way we as a society approach the questions? Do we also keep our eyes on the concerns of responsibility as we engage? What does the balance between these legitimate concerns look like? Biblical values are not to be pitted against each other but related to each other so both elements are honored. This is why cherry-picking between themes cannot be a biblical response.

I hope you are beginning to see how balancing extant tensions can work, as well as why these are topics that need the entire canon.

Faith and Work. This area is not so much about resolving a tension as seeing faith and work as important to pursue (though the tensions do surely surface once we walk into the often very secular workplace). Most church messages I hear largely bypass the 9 to 5, Monday through Friday part of the week. I hear a great deal on how to live at home, how to serve the church, how to share Jesus, how to manage the family, and how to think about the world. It's ironic that the workplace is so neglected, since it is often the place where we spend the bulk of our time. When the workplace is addressed, it may be only to ask how can we evangelize there and be a good witness.

Less talked about is how we should view work or how Scripture may help us with the challenges one faces there. Being a steward of the creation means understanding where work fits in. God has given us vocation in this life. How do we wrestle with the core tension between the sacred space we are a part of as members of God's people and the public space where we often spend most of our time serving? How do we face the ethical challenges in a pluralistic work space?

These last two questions do move us into tensions that Scripture addresses, but we only see them if we consider how Scripture handles such contexts. It is here that specific case studies covering a variety of challenging situations may help. Life-to-the-Bible application requires pastors and teachers who know the dilemmas people face from 9 to 5—a world many pastors or seminary faculty members have not been in. A commitment to speak on this topic requires getting to know your people and their activities in order to gain awareness about the questions involved.

World Religions. Here there are two sets of issues. The first is simply knowing what's out there. Most of us do not know enough about other religions to engage those who pursue them. This is where glocalization impacts us. It used to be that, to engage a neighbor, we only needed to understand another denomination or the difference between a Catholic or Protestant. In addition, there might have been an encounter with a Jewish person now and again. Now, though, between the way the world is linked technologically, how business is done globally, and the diversity of most contexts, that paradigm has changed. When it comes to world religions, most Christians think that all we need to know is how Christ is the answer and how our faith is the way. Those truths are essential and important, but is that all that is advised? No. We need to know more about the content of other faiths in order to engage them. Such understanding can open up additional ways of approaching someone with a different religious conviction.

Yet there is more. In this conversation, it's also valuable to try to understand what drives another faith and makes it attractive to people. What aspirations does it speak to and raise? How might the gospel step into that space? Here I have in mind trying to ask someone of a different faith what he or she senses it gives them and what causes a person to adhere to it. Is it the result of upbringing? Has it simply become a routine? Or is there something substantive that drives adherence that the gospel also treats, perhaps even more comprehensively? Knowing this might open up doors for us to address it.

Paul's speech in Acts 17 at Mars' Hill makes its challenge by acknowledging the draw of Greco-Roman spirituality, but then goes about addressing how the gospel fills that space—and does so even better. Books like Daniel help us see how a believer negotiates that other spiritual world (mainly by being who God calls us to be). Here the quality of our life is the draw versus trying to force a not-yet-appreciated lifestyle on others. Joseph shows the same approach to engagement in the book of Genesis, by focusing on his own integrity and his walk with the God of his people, rather than on dismantling the Egyptian system of deities. Books like Ezra demonstrate efforts to enforce moral standards, but interestingly, their focus is on how this is done "in house," among those who are connected to God. Do these distinct contexts have something to teach us as we seek to bring together all of what Scripture says about engagement in places where our neighbors do not share our faith? Does this distinction help us with governments that are not monoreligious?

Gun Control. This is a classic example of a category 3 issue. The tensions that come with this issue should give us pause about how to discuss it biblically. After all, guns did not exist when Scripture was written. We get to this topic in part by examining how Scripture handles violence. On the one hand, there are texts that allow me the right of self-defense (Exod 22:2; Num 35:5–13; Josh 20:4–6; Ps 72:12–14). Nations are allowed to bear the power of the sword (Rom 13:4). There are even OT laws that distinguish what happens if I kill someone who invades my tent at night versus my culpability if it happens during the day. In one instance there is no fine; in the other there may be (Exod 22:1–4). Distinctions like this begin to introduce our tension, which is the right to defend but with an awareness of how much violence to apply. Add to this the texts that plead for or describe non-violent responses, Jesus's general tenor toward dealing with violence, and the church's model of almost never fighting back with violence in the face of persecution—and we are suddenly in that space between tension and balance.

With this topic, cultural context also matters. In the UK, gun control is a different discussion than in the US because of cultural realities and different national laws about gun possession. In America, the right to own a gun is a constitutional "given." So the questions we discuss involve applying those rights in a way that is best for society at large. This is actually a complex question, especially in light of the biblical tensions just noted.

Part of my point in walking through these examples is to show how much room exists for discussion in category 2 and 3 topics. Usually in our ideological debates, the tension is bypassed for a choice. This actually robs us of discussions that the tensions suggest we need to have. We don't tend to ask how to balance the tensions or what their relationship might be as we seek to cope with it all. Yet the nature of the topic almost demands discussion. When the tensions are bypassed or go unrecognized altogether, we aren't aiding society's need to consider the real options that might exist.

Refugees and Immigration. Here is another category 3 topic that often is treated as a category 1. Its tensions are multiple. On the one side of the ledger is the right of a nation to establish its laws, expect them to be followed, and determine the kind of society it wishes to be. On the other side is the biblical call in many texts to have compassion for the alien and love one's neighbor.

Now, some try to adjudicate this by restricting who qualifies as the alien in Scripture, making it equivalent to a legal immigrant. I am not sure this works, given what Jesus taught. As we've seen, he dealt with the question of "Who is my neighbor?" and the call to be a neighbor in the parable of the Good Samaritan (Luke 10:28–38). According to Jesus, my call to love extends to anyone, even enemies (Luke 6:29–37). The tension remains.

This debate also often overlooks a little-appreciated aspect of our current situation: the moral responsibility we have applied to our laws. Our actions got us into this position to begin with: America invited people from other countries to work here initially, and we did not enforce immigration laws because we wanted the cheaper labor. This lasted for a few decades and produced a situation where those immigrants bore children with citizenship status and have never known another home besides America. How does our nation's moral responsibility for that relational and social reality impact our discussions in some of these cases?

Finally, as a democracy we have the option to look at how our laws are constructed with the opportunity to improve them. Such adjustments allow us to deal with the realities that our own actions have contributed to the problem. Add to this the layer of safety concerns tied to threats of terrorism, and the immigration question becomes far more complex, with multidimensional tensions.

Again, the approach of *life to the Bible* asks us to consider how to balance these factors by understanding what the realities are at various levels. Oversimplifying this discussion does no one any favors. No wonder this topic is so heavily discussed and hard to fully grasp. It requires slow, reflective thinking on all the biblical and social angles. The way in, I think, is not to deal with one of these dimensions only. That does not resolve all the tensions. Rather, we should face up to them all and enter into a deeper level of reflection.

Sexuality. My final example involves a category 1 issue. Some people might challenge the idea that same-sex issues are built on a core worldview difference, contending that Scripture at least holds open the possibility of monogamous same-sex relationships. Pursuing this argument within a biblical model, they claim that Scripture's condemnation of same-sex relationships is focused on specifically abusive relationships, such as a master and his unwilling slave. They also appeal to a "canceled" set of Old Testament precepts.

The biblical case for same-sex, monogamous relationships is not so strong. In Scripture there isn't a single mention of same-sex activity where it is expressed positively or even neutrally. It is always condemned or challenged. By the way, this recognition makes this discussion different than debates on slavery or the activity of women. In those two discussions, a canonical look at texts shows pro and con elements that need to be balanced. The biblical evidence also means the slavery/women/same-sex analogy does not work. In fact, some who favor same-sex relationships simply concede that to advocate for monogamous same-sex marriage means one has to argue that the Bible is wrong in prohibiting it. That recognition says a lot about the topic and what the Bible does teach. It also shows the honesty of some who contend for this alternative lifestyle that some do actually recognize what they are contending for is not what the Bible teaches versus others who claim it does permit such cases.

This topic is a straightforward, category 1, worldview clash. To get there, a person has to cancel out or challenge the reality that every time this topic comes up biblically, it is in a context where the behavior is rebuked.

In the area of sexuality, the tensions are not so much biblical as practical, pastoral, and applicational. We have national laws that allow for a lifestyle that is not biblically sanctioned, and even laws at levels that prohibit discrimination. Here the tension is between the world and the biblical ethic. This is but one space where the world and Scripture run into each other. Beyond this obvious practical tension, there is still more.

Despite the seeming biblical clarity, there are tensions at a pastoral level as well. Pastoral tensions arise anytime the commitment to minister to people and help them grow spiritually and morally intersects with someone's immoral behavior. Debate exists as to whether homosexual sin, because it is against the nature of things, is more severe in its impact than other sins or is just a particularly vivid example in Romans 1. Tensions here become obvious when sins that are rooted in heterosexual misbehavior are handled by the church one way, while same-sex sins are treated another way. Should this be? To chastise one category of sin while being more "sympathetic" to another category may be evidence of how cherry-picking can happen. It also undercuts the impact and the morality of the church on issues at a pastoral and relational level.

On the other hand, how does a pastor maintain the corporate concerns and testimony of the church while seeking to minister to anyone caught in moral failure? How does a shepherd attempt to lead individuals into growth?

Biblical texts point to both nurture and discipline as means for the church to use. The tensions are resolving how, how much, and when. These texts talk about the contextual sphere of the church. What does one argue for in a public space where both moral (i.e., spiritual) enablement and a moral restriction may be lacking? Understandable concerns for the well-being of society drive our efforts to engage the full public context and challenge such a lifestyle, but theological and relational understanding may make one aware of the challenges that come with it. Here expectations may need calibrating alongside a reminder of where real solutions lie. Those limited expectations need to include a recognition that a person's ultimate accountability is to God, regardless of our national laws. Each person becomes accountable before God for their choices, no matter what the laws of the land may be.

My point in raising this example is to show how tensions may help us with a discussion. How we balance these tensions still needs to be sorted out, and the specific context may matter significantly in such a discussion. Responsibility in the church should work differently and demand more than expectations in the world at large. The character and purity of church values are in view here, along with the need to show moral life in the church. Its values are not like the values of the world.

There also is the pastoral concern of wrestling with how to work compassionately with those caught in sin. Scripture suggests that the community of faith only leave them on their own when they show no desire to consider living differently (Matt 18:15–18). No wonder the church has been challenged with how to approach this area of sexual sin while maintaining its moral commitments.

Conclusion on Examples

What I have attempted to do with these examples is to open a dialogue on how life-to-the-Bible discussions might work, especially with regard to the kinds of questions they ask about text and setting. Obviously, what the Bible says is key, even in working backwards from life to the Bible. The point is that bringing the Bible to that discussion has to be canonical and contextual, not merely exegetical or expositional.

An introductory overview to the examples and challenges we face does not answer all the questions a person might have. Instead, it raises questions for reflection. My goal has been to suggest what these discussions look like at the start. Only a full treatment of each theme according to such an approach would move a person closer to specific kinds of answers. That is not just another book, but another set of books beyond our scope. But I do hope to have shown where to start. I also hope to have laid some biblical rationale for why, in many cases, we must go into these spaces to show cultural intelligence.

May this be the beginning of a long-needed, important discussion about how we apply Scripture and live the life God calls for from all of us.

Summarizing Cultural Intelligence

Cultural intelligence requires us to understand our assignment. People are not the enemy. They are the goal. As we engage, it's important to appreciate that our battle is spiritual and people are caught in the grasp of forces they often do not even recognize. We need to understand that real change is not a matter of law or politics but of spiritual transformation that only the hope of the gospel can give. That realization might help the church to emphasize what can bring real change and lessen the emotion that often comes in our political debates. The culture war's elevation of politics to a more central role has not served the church well. It has distracted us from our core mission as a church, obscuring what we should care about the most: the message of how the gospel is the best way to meet human need.

Tone also matters in cultural engagement. Paul shows us that whatever we may think about culture, engaging requires working to build bridges. The texts on dealing with people outside the church call us to be gentle, gracious, and humble as we challenge. The effort to engage requires balancing challenge and invitation. We are never to lose sight of the fact that hope is our core emphasis. In the debates that are often a part of engagement, we don't desire to leave biblical conviction behind or fail to express it, but how we do this needs recalibration in many settings, as does what we prioritize. The opportunity to learn by listening well may also be a healthy by-product of seeking to listen more carefully as we engage.

Intelligent engagement will lead us into many challenging and difficult discussions. We need to patiently and diligently listen—and listen well—for those bridges to hope.

We need to appreciate the complexity of life in a fallen world. Recognizing real biblical tensions of fallen-world life may help us have discussions that move beyond labels to substance.

The most important way to open doors to hope may be showing the authenticity the Bible contains about life. We can do this by what we say, and especially by how we say and live it. Cultural intelligence reflects a commitment to love others well, including those outside the church. We seek by the power of the Spirit to draw outsiders toward an invitation to faith. It requires an ability to switch-hit: going from the Bible to life or working from life to draw people back to the Bible.

Cultural intelligence also involves an appreciation of the richness of Scripture, discernment, and dependence on the leading of God. It means grasping the core elements of our call. They involve a spiritual battle and the capability of the gospel to enhance life and allow it to flourish for those who believe. Christians are ambassadors for Christ in the world. Our citizenship is a heavenly one that transcends our national commitments. We are commissioned to represent God individually and together as the church. We should do so with applied intelligence in the spaces and places God has us. We do so through an invitation into hope and into a new and different kind of life—an entry into sacred space in the midst of life in the public space. That life is lived out because of grace, forgiveness, reconnection to God, and enablement from God's Spirit, which is given to those who turn to him in faith.

A spiritual challenge requires spiritual resources and a way of engagement unlike that of the world (Eph 6:10–18). I close with the reminder of 2 Tim 2:24–26, for in it is a glimpse of how to engage with cultural intelligence. This text summarizes hope and a spiritual prayer of practical guidance for the way forward:

> The Lord's servant must not quarrel, but must be gentle to everyone, able to teach, and patient, instructing his opponents with gentleness. Perhaps God will grant them repentance leading them to the knowledge of the truth. Then they may come to their senses and escape the trap of the devil, who has taken them captive to do his will.

INDEX